Growin' up Country:
Rural Life in the 1950's and 1960's

By: J. Everett Moore Jr.

Growin' up Country: Rural Life in the 1950's and 1960's

By. J. Everett Moore Jr.

Publisher: Springfield Historic
Preservation, LLC

Copyright 2012
LCCN
2012908427
ISBN
978-0-9855999-0-4

Growin' up Country:
Rural Life in the 1950's and 1960's

CONTENTS

I.	ACKNOWLEDGMENTS	
II.	FOREWORD	
III.	BRIEF HISTORY	15
IV.	HOME	27
V.	RECREATION	37
VI.	MOORE BROTHERS	47
VII.	WORK/CHORES	53
VIII.	CHURCH	69
IX.	WALL'S HOMESTEAD	77
X.	JIMMIE'S	93
XI.	SCHOOL	99
XII.	WILSON'S STORE	109
XIII.	HOLIDAYS	115
XIV.	GARDENS	121
XV.	MEALS/TRADITIONAL FOODS	125
XVI.	MEDICAL	131
XVII.	TELEPHONE	137
XVIII.	RADIO	141
XIX.	NEWSPAPERS	145

XX.	TELEVISION	149
XXI.	MAIL	155
XXII.	TRANSPORTATION	159
XXIII.	SEGREGATION/INTEGRATION	165
XXIV.	ACCENTS	169
XXV.	MEMORABLE EVENTS	172
	a. HURRICANE HAZEL	173
	b. MARCH '62 STORM	174
	c. HARRINGTON FAIR	175
	d. ROCKET SLED	176
	e. GROUND HOG	177
	f. BEAVER DAM	178
	g. RETURN DAY	179
	h. INDIAN RIVER BRIDGE COLLAPSE	182
XXVI.	LORE/TALES/TIDBITS/BRIEF NOTES	184
	a. BRAWN	184
	b. THE HUNTER	185
	c. FIRE WHISTLE	185
	d. BURNT SWAMP	186
	e. GEORGETOWN DEMONSTRATION SCHOOL	187

	f.	LITTLE ENGINE THAT COULD	188
	g.	FOX HUNTING	189
	h.	NOXZEMA	190
	i.	DUNKARDS	191
XXVII.		SAYINGS/EXPRESSIONS/PROVERBS	192
XXVIII.		APPENDICES	196
	I	FAMILY TREE	196
	II	POP POP'S POETRY	202
	III	HISTORY OF ST. JOHN'S CHURCH	206
	IV	MOM'S RECIPES	214

ACKNOWLEDGMENTS

This book is possible due to the encouragement and assistance of many. I am grateful that my parents instilled in me a love of history and encouraged my study of our local history and lore. This love of history was nurtured by Frank Hewitt, my seventh grade U.S History teacher, who made history fun. Local author and historian, Dr. William Williams, was a tremendous influence during my college years as his student and beyond college as a friend. Even though he is gone, his influence lives on. My uncle, Carlton Moore, was of tremendous assistance in filling in the gaps of my memory and answering my many questions. Jimmie Truitt answered many questions and made sure my farming and neighborhood recollections were correct. Ronnie Dodd is always an excellent resource for local history and lore. There are so many others that have added their suggestions.

A special thanks to Clarke White for allowing access to his special collection on the poultry industry, to Di Rafter and the Agricultural Museum and Village, Bill Dimondi at the Delaware State Fair, Tom Draper and the staff at WBOC, and John Hoebee for their help in finding pictures and materials.

The Marvel Museum in Georgetown is a real gem and should be on a must see list for any local history buffs. Thanks to Rosalee Walls and Jim Bowden for their assistance.

Also thanks to the Hagley Museum and Library, The University of Delaware Morris Library, and the Delaware State Archives for their assistance and help. Thanks to Don Dwyer for proof reading and his professional guidance (his punctuation suggestions added five pounds and 10 pages to this book).

I also thank all those who have published local history books before me, including my friends, Russ McCabe, the late Aubrey Murray, Secretary of Agriculture Edwin (Ed) Kee, and William (Bill) Wade to name a few. A special thank you goes to Dick Carter not only for his contributions in preserving our history but for being there with encouragement and advice.

One person whose assistance has been invaluable and deserves special credit is

Stacy Ponshock. Stacy was a student of the Communications Department at Delaware Technical & Community College in Georgetown and was able to figure out the publishing software that was much smarter than I. Her work in the office, as well as response to e-mails and questions enabled this book to be completed in a timely manner.

During the final stages of my book, I suffered eye retina detachments which necessitated surgery on six occasions and which slowed the process of finishing the book. I would like to thank Dr. Carl Maschauer of Sussex Eye Center, Dr. John Butler of Delmarva Retina Associates and his staff, and Dr. Camporchiaro of the Wilmer Eye Institute at Johns Hopkins for their contributions in saving my eyesight.

I thank you all.

DEDICATED TO MY CHILDREN, JENNY, LARA, JAIME, TREY

WHO NOW WILL SEE IN PRINT THE STORIES THEY HAVE HEARD
OVER THE YEARS

AND TO MY GRANDCHILDREN,

ADDISON AND BRYNLEE

THE NEIGHBORHOOD IN THE MID-1950'S

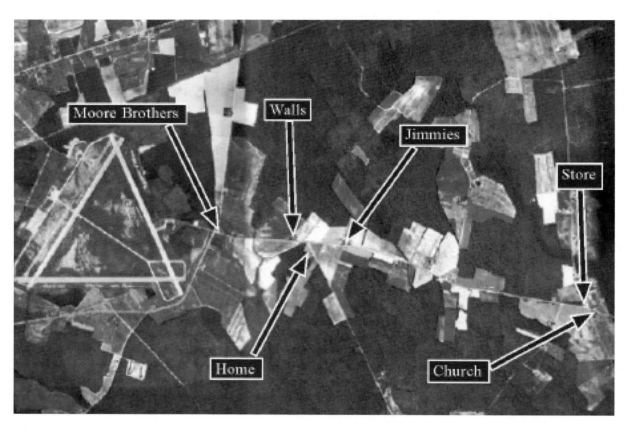

This map shows the neighborhood from the airport along Springfield Road to Wilson's Store and the Church. Also shown are Home, Wall's Homestead, and Jimmie's.

Foreword

In starting this project my goal was simple...to give people a glimpse of what it was like growing up in rural America in the 1950s and 1960s.

It was a time of few divorces (I only knew of one divorced family while in elementary school), no hyphenated Americans (our neighborhood was all WASP), few, if any, credit cards, and no lawsuits. In fact, as a young child I asked Mom what it meant to sue someone, and she responded that "it is something that good people do not do." It was also the time period that marked the beginning of the space race from Sputnik to Apollo Eleven's landing on the moon.

Over the years, many people have moved into our area that do not know our history and lore and what it was like to live here just a few years ago. As one whose families have lived here for generations,[1] I often find myself telling stories of our heritage and history and have found that many enjoy hearing those stories.

The setting is a very small geographical area east of Georgetown, Delaware, that often was referred to as "St. Johns" or "St. John's neighborhood" (for the Church).

In addition to recounting childhood memories, I have also added the histories of certain areas of interest, e.g., Wilson's Store and St. Johns Church, etc. Although I do provide traditional histories of these, most of the history I recite is at best an anecdotal history based on my observations and local lore. There are many good histories of Sussex County and my chapter entitled "Brief History" is just that...brief...and is added for context for those who are unfamiliar with or new to the area. I have also recounted stories and the way of doing things prior to my time. These are added because they were part of the everyday lore and conversations.

---

1. See Appendix A for the authors genealogy.

As I wrote, one recurring theme became apparent that I did not think of before I started writing. In this day of the discussion of carbon caps and recycling we recycled and saved things as a matter of course... and it was not for environmental reasons....it was part of the normal frugality of the times.

What did occur to me was the simpler time in which we lived. I think it is best stated in an Eulogy I gave on February 10,1994, at the death of Jimmie Truitt, Sr. I stated:

> *"When I think of Jimmie Truitt, I think of a way of life. To me he represented a simpler, easier-going time when everybody had time for everyone else. A time when people visited and talked. A time when there was plenty of room to roam, wander and hunt without disturbing others. A time when it was safe for kids to roam the neighborhood, knowing that the neighbors knew them and would care for them."*

That is the world I knew as a child.

Brief History

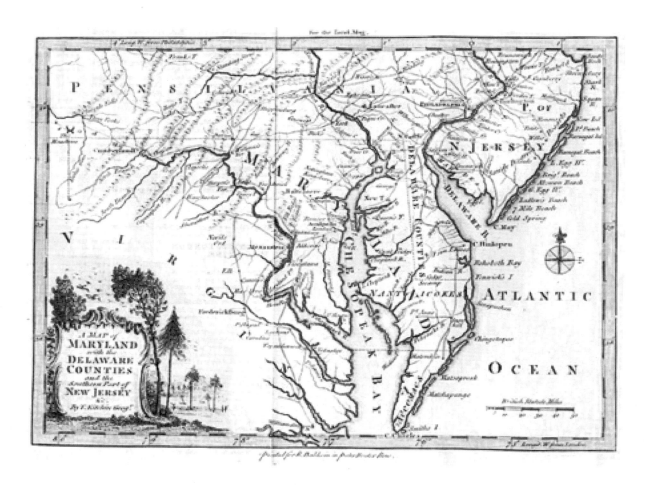

Until the Revolution, many maps continued to show Delaware as part of Pennsylvania, even though they rebelled at being part of Pennsylvania in 1704 and started their own assembly - thus creating Delaware. In this map, Delaware is shown as the "Delaware Counties." Others of the same period refer to Delaware as the "Lower Three Counties." Map courtesy of mapsofpa.com

Brief History

The events in this book take place in the Mid-Atlantic region of the country in the state of Delaware. Delaware is a small state with only three Counties. Sussex County, the lifelong home of the author and his family, is the southern most and largest (by area) of the counties.

Sussex County, Delaware is bounded on the east by the Atlantic Ocean and the Delaware Bay, on the south and west by the eastern shore of Maryland, and on the north by Kent County, Delaware. Sussex County, the largest and widest of Delaware's three counties, is 35 miles wide at its widest point along its southern border with Maryland.

This is the Mason Dixon marker that is found at the Southwest corner of the state of Delaware, west of Delmar, DE, off of Route 54. Photo courtesy of Delaware Public Archives.

The Delaware Bay and River were first explored by the English explorer, Henry Hudson, on his Dutch commissioned ship, The Half Moon, in 1609. In 1610, the river and bay, and the Indians that inhabited their shores were named in honor of Lord De La Warr, the first royal governor of Virginia.

Sussex County—and, in fact, our state—was first settled by the Dutch in the area now known as Lewes, but then called Zwaanendale in 1631. Although the Swedes next governed Delaware, there is little evidence of this in Sussex.

Growin' Up Country

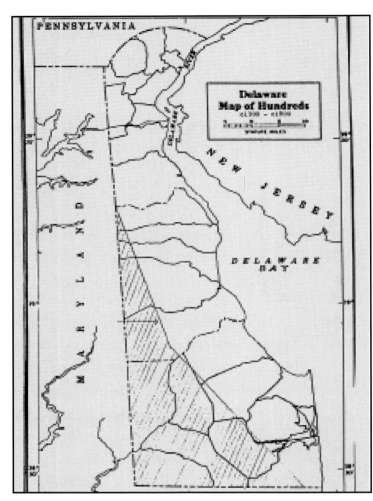

A Hundreds map of Delaware showing that portion of Delaware (the hatched area) claimed by Maryland prior to the Mason Dixon line. Photo courtesy of Delaware Public Archives.

In 1760, the surveyors, Charles Mason and Jeremiah Dixon, were hired to settle the boundary dispute, thence the Mason-Dixon line.

The European settlers did encounter Indians when they arrived in the new world. The Indians of Sussex County were not Delaware Indians, who resided more to the north. They were named for the river...not the state. Several tribes inhabited Sussex County. The Nanticokes occupied the area from Concord and Seaford area west to the Chesapeake Bay along the Nanticoke River. A large contingent of Nanticokes bought land and now reside in the Oak Orchard area along the Indian River Bay. Choptank Indians were also thought to inhabit western Sussex. The central and eastern areas of Sussex were inhabited by Assateague's, Indian River Indians and other small tribes and groups of Indians.

The English came next. Many know that Delaware was once referred to as the Lower Three Counties of Pennsylvannia. What many do not know is that much of Sussex County was once claimed by Maryland. Pennsylvania was controlled by the Penns, and Maryland was controlled by the Calverts. Maryland claimed that portion of Sussex that ran approximately from north of Greenwood to just west of Fenwick Island. In fact, much of Dagsboro and the area south and west was given to General John Dagsworthy (for whom the town is named) by the Lord Calvert of Maryland.

Like most coastal areas along the Mid-Atlantic, Sussex County is crisscrossed by many rivers, creeks, and streams that at one time supplied the power for local grist mills. Though the names of many towns today reflect this important heritage, such as Milton, Millsboro, and Milford, it wasn't just towns that had grist mills. They dotted the countryside wherever a small stream and a settlement of people intersected.

Rural Life in the 1950's and 60's

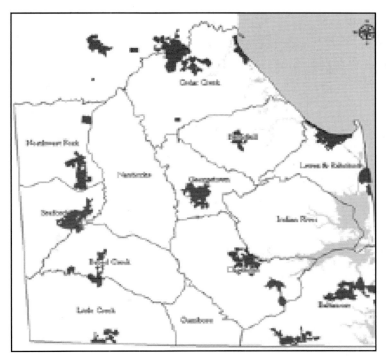

This is a map of the "Hundreds" of Sussex County as they exist today. They are still used in legal downtown and for taxation purposes.

These same waterways allowed shipbuilding to be a thriving industry in Sussex. There were three shipyards on the Broadkill River in and around Milton, three on the Misspillion in and around Milford, a shipyard in Bethel, and a shipyard in Seaford.

Delaware is one of the few states that recognizes the political subdivisions known as "Hundreds." There is some dispute as to the original meaning of the term, but the most widely accepted definition is that area in which 100 families resided. Hundreds are still in use and can be found on legal descriptions on deeds and for tax purposes.

The original Hundreds of Sussex County were Baltimore, Broadkiln (now referred to as Broadkill), Broad Creek, Cedar Creek, Dagsborough, (now spelled Dagsboro), Georgetown, Indian River, Lewes and Rehoboth, Little Creek, Nanticoke, and Northwest Fork Hundreds. Two more hundreds, Gumboro and Seaford, were added later.

Over the years, the State has had many nicknames...The Diamond State, a name given by Thomas Jefferson; The Blue Hen State, for the penchant of our troops in the Revolution to conduct cock fights with our fighting Blue Hen chickens; The Peach State, because of the amount of peaches grown; and The First State because we were the first state to ratify the Constitution. Most recently it is referred to as "The Small Wonder" due to its small size and many benefits.

The Blue Hen Rooster. During the Revolutionary War the Delaware troops, particularly from Kent County, were known for their penchant of cock fights with the Blue Hen Chicken. The Roosters were very tenacious and the troops often exhibited the same tenacity. As a result our troops were often referred to as the Fighting Blue Hens.

Growin' Up Country

Lewes was the first capital of Sussex County but the capital was moved to Georgetown on January 29, 1791, per an Act of the General Assembly. Since so much land was added to the county when the dispute with Maryland was settled, Georgetown became the county seat because it was too inconvenient for those on the western part of the county to travel all the way to Lewes by horseback to conduct county business and to vote. Georgetown was located in an area referred to as James Pettyjohn's Old Field, which was deemed to be the central location of Sussex County.

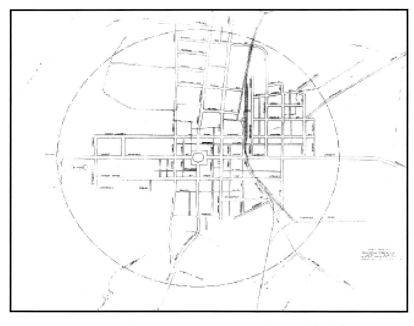

A map of Georgetown prior to recent annexations that changed its traditional circle shape. The town limits were a 1/2 mile radius from the center of the circle. Photo courtesy of Delaware Public Archives.

Traditionally, towns and villages were near navigable rivers or streams. This was not the case with Georgetown. The location was selected solely because it was located geographically in the center of the County.

This area was wilderness. Just a few generations ago, the deed to my brother's property, a few miles east of Georgetown, referred to his lands as being located in "the wilderness of Indian River Hundred."

The roads that existed through the area were really just cart paths that were nothing more than deep ruts cut by wagon wheels and were often impassible in wet weather or after freezes and thaws of the winter. My mother often commented that even in the 1920s she had nightmares about the poor condition of the roads and her fears of being stuck in the road miles from the nearest neighbor.

During the Civil War, we were considered a border state. Though we remained with the Union, there were many Confederate sympathizers, especially in downstate Delaware. Delaware did not have a state-wide militia, and many joined militias in neighboring states until Delaware organized its own three regiments. An ancestor of the author, Dagworthy Joseph, was one such individual who joined the Union forces in Maryland and ended the war as a colonel. He later received a Presidential Commission as keeper of the locally famous Henlopen Lighthouse.

Rural Life in the 1950's and 60's

Railroads came to the area after the Civil War, not just for travel, but more importantly for the transport of goods to market. This truly allowed the markets for our produce and seafoods to flourish. A review of old maps reveals such names as Bennum's Switch, Salisbury Switch and others. These were railroad sidings where local farmers and merchants loaded their goods for the market, often to distant cities such as Wilmington, Philadelphia, and Baltimore. As a child, I heard many conversations peppered with references to these long-gone landmarks.

Dagworthy Joseph, great, great grandfather of the author was the longest serving caretaker of the Henlopen light house. He fought for the Union in the Civil War having joined the militia in Maryland. Photo courtesy of Delaware Digital Postcard Collection, University of Delaware Library, Newark, Delaware.

The area is historically Protestant, and of that Protestant faith, predominately Methodist. In fact, Barrett's Chapel, located in Kent County, is known as "The Cradle of Methodism." This is the result of a meeting between John Asbury and Thomas Coke that took place there prior to the conference in Baltimore, Maryland, in which the Methodist Episcopal Church was organized. Due to the poor travel conditions in the Colonies, many did not attend churches. Instead, the ministers traveled to the people and held camp meetings which many people from the area attended. Many local Churches continued the tradition of camp meetings held usually outdoors in the summer. The most prominent one that still continues the tradition today is Carey's Camp.

Several of our resorts started as religious retreats for Protestant denominations. Rehoboth and Fenwick were both Methodist Camp meeting locations, and Bethany started as a non-denominational Protestant camp meeting site. In fact, alcohol could not be served in Bethany until 1985, when the Court struck down the old prohibitions against alcohol.

Barrett's Chapel near Frederica in Kent County is known as the "Cradle of Methodism". Photo ccurtesy of Delaware Digital Postcard Collection, University of Delaware Library, Newark, Delaware.

Growin' Up Country

During WWII towers were erected along the Atlantic beaches to protect the mouth of the Delaware Bay. They stand today as stark reminders of the fear that once gripped our country. Photo courtesy of Sam Ellis Photography.

During World War II, the area was abuzz with Civil Defense activities. Our coastal areas were patrolled and lookout towers still stand which were manned watching for U-boats during the war. Fort Miles at Cape Henlopen was part of our national defense network as was the newly established naval air station in Georgetown.

Due to new comers to the area during both the Depression and World War II, a Catholic parish was established in Georgetown in 1956. The parish served not just Georgetown, but also Milton and Millsboro areas. After the war, a new industry started that not only changed our immediate area but also the entire peninsula...that being the poultry or broiler industry. In 1923, Mrs. Wilmer Steele received 500 chicks from her supplier instead of the 50 she ordered. She raised them and sold them for 69 cents per pound live weight, which provided a substantial profit. Traditionally, chickens were raised for their eggs and then eaten by the owner after the most productive egg producing period had passed. Our area still has more chickens than people and has more chickens per capita than any place in the world, growing 200 million chickens per year.

Georgetown is known for its "Circle" in the center of town. In fact, the town itself was a circle with the boundaries being one-half mile from the center of the circle. The town was thus one mile across at all points. Interestingly, many of the old-timers referred not to the "Circle" but to the "Square," based on the outer perimeter.

Since Georgetown is the County Seat, many governmental offices of Sussex County, the State, and Federal Governments are located in town. During the time frame of this book, the County did not have "home rule" and was governed by a Levy Court.

Mrs. Wilmer (Cecil) Steele in front of her chicken houses. She is credited with starting the poultry industry. Photo courtesy of Delaware Agricultural Museum and Village.

Rural Life in the 1950's and 60's

The Court House dominates the Circle by its sheer size and height. It houses the State Courts and during the time frame of the book also housed the County offices such as the Clerk of Peace, Register of Wills, Recorder of Deeds, Register in Chancery, Sheriff, and the Prothonotary. Photo courtesy of Delaware Digital Postcard Collection, University of Delaware Library, Newark, Delaware.

Note the caption on the margin that refers to the postcard as being of the "PUBLIC SQUARE". It is now universally referred to as the "Circle". Photo from the author's collection.

The Farmers Bank building stood on the southwest corner of the Circle and South Bedford Street. It added an imposing and elegant presence to the Circle for many years. Photo courtesy of Delaware Digital Postcard Collection, University of Delaware Library, Newark, Delaware.

Rural Life in the 1950's and 60's

The Brick Hotel has been a prominent feature on The Circle since 1836. During the Civil War it was reported that the Brick Hotel was a favorite hang out of Union sympathizers. From the 1960's until 1999, the building was used as a Wilmington Trust Bank. It is now reopened as the Brick Hotel, a popular Inn and restaurant owned and operated by Lynn and Ed Lester. Photo courtesy of University of Delaware Digital Postcard Collection, University of Delaware Library, Newark, Delaware.

"The Circle"
by: George T. Russell

You say you are a stranger
And you wish to look around
Well, you'll find we have a Circle
In the center of our town.

It wasn't always called this name
It once was called the Square
Way back when homes lined every side
But they're no longer there.

The Town Hall, banks, the postal place
The Courthouse standing tall
Some businesses, some offices
Now occupy most all.

It started as a crossing place
Where Indians once met
And, if the white man hadn't come
I guess they'd be there yet.

But come he did and he built homes
And filled the land nearby
Yes, it was just a tiny place
In seventeen ought five.

The years went by, the place it grew
And then in ninety-one
A group said, "Let us start a town"
And that's how it begun.

They tell the tale there was no sale
Of the land where the Circle stands
But was given free to always be
A park for you and me.

Many strange things have happened there
So I've heard by way of mouth
How young men learned to march there
When the north, it fought the south.

Then years ago when news was slow
And most folks couldn't read`
They would come here on Return Day
The Town Crier's words to heed.

Standing on the Courthouse balcony
He would shout so all could hear,
And learn who had been elected
At the voting held that year.

They would cook within the Circle
And sell things which they had made
Like cider, quilts and pies and cakes
And they would even trade.

The horses and the oxen
Would be tethered near the Square
And the folks would have a picnic
While they were gathered there.

Politicians have stood beneath these trees
And spouted words so wise
But as we look back, in retrospect
We find that most were lies.

Nearby once stood the "whipping post,"
A grim thing to behold
Thirty lashes on your back you'd get
If some chickens you had stole.

Today "The Post" it is no more
New Laws, they now prevail
And if you rob somebody's home
They put you into jail.

Rural Life in the 1950's and 60's

The jails are filled to bursting
They don't know what to do
The crime rate rises every day
What tact shall they pursue?

Today my mind goes back in time
I remember oh so clear
How the firemen held a carnival
At the Circle every year.

A "ferris wheel," a "carousel"
Would grace that hollowed spot
And I would wonder at it all
When I was just a tot.

The lights would gleam in the darkness
The music would sound so grant
I would feel as tho I was marching
To John Phillip Sousa's Band.

A nickel I'd bet at the blanket stand
The last one that I had
And when my number didn't win
I'd feel so very sad.

Today some things are missing
At the Circle in the Square
And there are few that remember
That they were ever there.

The "horse trough" made of metal
The bandstand gleaming white
And gas lights flickering all around
To light your way at night.

Yes, times will change and memories dim
And we shall pass away
But the Circle on and on shall go
I hope till "Judgement Day."

George T. Russell, author of "The Circle". George was the great uncle of the author (his grandmother's brother) and often submitted poetry to the local paper, The Sussex Countian. He was a wounded war veteran and known locally as a spittin' image of country music and TV star, Tennessee Ernie Ford. Photo courtesy of Carlton R. Moore

Home

This is the home located on Deep Branch Road that Mom and Dad bought when they were 18, and where Mom lived for 69 years until her death. Photo by the author.

Home

I often have the opportunity to discuss my childhood. I refer to it as an Ozzie & Harriet type childhood, but we didn't live in town and Dad didn't wear a suit.

My earliest memories revolve around Church and family. As more fully detailed later, the Church played a large part in our life—Sunday School, Preaching, M.Y.F. (Methodist Youth Fellowship), Bible School, Homecoming, and Ice Cream Festivals all provided activities for our small close knit community.

I was third in a family of three boys and a younger sister. Ronald, the oldest, was 12 years older than I—he actually started college when I started the first grade. Merrill was six years older than I and started Junior High when I started first grade. Teresa, the youngest and only girl, was four years younger than I and the only one of us born in the hospital. Although we were not unlike other families in our neighborhood, I do believe Mom and Dad—especially Mom — probably emphasized education more than most. One of her favorite sayings was that "education is something no one can take from you." We were constantly told that "you can be whatever you want to be." Hard work, education and a dream was all we needed.

The Moore family, circa 1955. Seated left to right, are Ronald, Teresa, being held by the our father, J. Everett Moore, Sr. or, in the neighborhood parlance, "Big Everett," our mother, Dorothy, Merrill, and me. Photo from author's collection.

Growin' Up Country

We lived on a dirt road, County Road No. 315, now called Deep Branch Road[1], east of Georgetown, in Sussex County, Delaware, in a two-story, three-bedroom, one-bath farmhouse. There was no central heat or air conditioning—in fact, I didn't know anyone with central heat or air. The house was heated by three space heaters downstairs with no heat upstairs. In the summer, we slept with the windows open and had a window fan to move the air. We were fortunate to have one air conditioner in the living room, and on extremely hot nights, I sometimes sneaked down and slept on the floor in the air conditioned room. In the winter, we slept with plenty of handmade quilts for warmth. The quilts made us warm and toasty, but our feet moved quickly in the mornings when they touched the cold linoleum floor. We quickly scrambled downstairs to the heat.

Some may have a romantic image of living on a dirt road, but it did have its drawbacks. Road graders periodically scraped the road to fill in the pot holes and to fix the "washboard" surface of the road. During the winter freezes and thaws, the road became unstable and it was not unheard of for people to get stuck. Obviously, it was very messy during rainstorms or snowstorms. In the dry summers, dust came into the house with each passing car. The wash on the clothes lines also got dusty. The State Highway Department spread calcium on that section of the roads in front of houses to keep the dust down.

My parents purchased the farm shortly after the birth of my oldest brother, Ronald. They paid $900.00 in 1939 for 90-plus acres and the home. At the time of my mother's death in 2008, she had lived there for 69 years.

I really do not think my life or that of my family was much different from those of other rural and farm families around the country at that time. Like many farms in Sussex County, ours had some chicken houses around the house, and we raised Black Angus cattle. The cattle we raised were beef cattle, so there was no milking operation. We did have pastures, a corral and a loading dock. By the time I started school, we no longer raised cattle or chickens. We rented or allowed someone to till our land on shares. Dad was

Ours was a close knit family with aunts, uncles, cousins, and extended family all within a short distance. Birthdays were eagerly anticipated because it meant the extended family got together to celebrate. From left to right; me, my sister, Teresa, and cousin Lynn.

---

1. As a boy the road was referred to as "New Road". In the 1868 Beers Atlas, Road 315 from route 47 to its intersection with 317 was not in existence.. It appears that section was built sometime in the early 1900s. Hence the name "New Road". It remained a dirt road until I was in the fifth grade.

Rural Life in the 1950's and 60's

heavily involved in the business, known as Moore Brothers, described in a later chapter.

Although Deep Branch Road is now loaded with homes—86 to be exact-—at that time it only had nine homes. From north to south these homes were: our family, Mr. and Mrs. Harvey Breisch, who retired here from the city, Will and Lorraine Rogers, Alvin and Minnie Wilson, Aunt Maime Thompson, Oliver Adkins, Clyde and Lizzie Andrews, George and Edna Layton, and the Joe Hylinski family. Springfield Road (route 47), which we always referred to as the main road, now has 11 new homes that were not there when I was a youth. That is a total of 88 new homes on just two of the roads of my childhood world.

The area looked different then. Many of the grain fields we see now were pastures for beef and milk cows. The fields were smaller with hedge rows between the fields. Those hedge rows were perfect nesting places for a wide assortment of birds and small animals.

Many of the homes had chicken houses, barns, and other farm buildings near the house. Most had gardens and many had chickens running loose in the yard.[2] Some of the old timers did not have grass in their yards because the chickens or other animals kept the grass from growing. Others painted all the trees white up to a certain height.... normally shoulder high. Those same families might have old tires half buried upright and painted white to outline the driveway or entrance to the yard.

After supper, families often visited their neighbors. There was no invitation or phone call in advance. Adults talked about the crops, the weather, and the local or regional news while the children played. It was traditional for a snack to be served to the visitors. When we visited in the summer, we often sat on the front porch, usually on rockers. The quiet was occasionally interrupted by the small talk of the adults, the sound of the children (always

Many in rural areas painted trees, poles, and posts white. I am unaware of any practical purpose but was done for aesthetic reasons only. Photo by the author.

referred to as "the kids") playing with the neighbor's dog[3] or chasing fireflies (referred to as "lightening bugs"), or the sound of the occasional passing car.

Living in the country with such a small population in the County back then, we rarely saw a car we didn't recognize. If we visited

---

2. These were the chickens for the families' own use for eggs or food. They would be referred to as "free range chickens" today.
3. Everyone had a dog and some cats. They were normally outdoor pets only and the cats were slangily referred to as "mousers". They were kept outside to keep the mouse population down in the barns and sheds

the neighbors and sat on their porch, we often knew who was passing by just by the time of night or by the sound or the speed of the vehicle.

Other nights, we watched some TV, talked, or played games. Our conversations usually centered around Mom and Dad's childhood or experiences as young adults. Dad often told of a mule he purchased as a young man, and how he had difficulty plowing or cultivating with that mule. When he was going in a direction away from the house, it was difficult to keep the mule pulling. He laughed as he recounted how the mule reacted when he turned back in the direction toward home. Dad struggled to hold the mule as it ran toward the stables. Obviously, it did not want to work the fields. Dad quickly sold that mule.

Many shops had posters such as the one above showing different hairstyles of the time.

Shops had posters advertising the different hair tonics and creams. Brylcream and Wildroot were two popular hair creams of the time. Please note the traditional barber pole in the poster.

When we played games, it usually was "comey-comey," a game Mom played when she was young. Mom usually started the game by saying "comey-comey." We responded by saying, "what do you come by?" She then responded with a letter. We then had to answer with an inanimate object in the room that started with that letter. We all shouted out guesses until someone guessed the word. The winner then picked a letter for others to guess.

Our lives were very peaceful and quiet. We saw and heard no more than a handful of cars per day and saw and heard very few aircraft. Televisions were not blaring all day and the radio was on only for news or special

Rural Life in the 1950's and 60's

This is the Clover Farm Store on the corner of North Bedford and Bramhall Streets where my mother did our grocery shopping when I was a child. It was owned by Mr. and Mrs. Lloyd Rogers. Mrs. Rogers often sent home a small bag of penny candy for my sister and me when Mom shopped there. The store was most recently known as 3 Bears Nursery. Please note the telephone booth on the exterior of the building. Photo courtesy of Gerry Hammond, grandson of Mr. and Mrs. Rogers.

mirrors with different brands of hair tonic so that the patron could use their favorite brand to hold their hair in place. Our brand was Vitalis. The whole experience was more of a social gathering than a chore that had to be done. There were magazines and comics to keep one occupied while waiting, and the men usually talked about the topic of the day. The haircuts were traditional men's style, tapered to the top and cut over the ear. Some even had flat tops and buzz cuts like Merrill and I had one summer in the mid 50's. The buzz cuts were called a "teaberry whiz."

farm reports. It was a time when people saw no need to lock their homes, cars, or churches.

We had minimal contact with anyone outside our rural area. Prior to getting my driver's license, I rarely visited Dover or Salisbury, Maryland.[4] If my family ventured out of Georgetown for shopping, it was north to Milford. Usually there was no need to leave our community. Many in the neighborhood even had their hair cut by a family member instead of going to town for a haircut. We went to the barber shop in town for haircuts. No man at the time dared go to a beauty salon. The barber shops were operated on a first come first serve basis with no appointments. Shelves lined the

Although officially "Purnell's Hardware," everyone just called it Purnell's. It had all kinds of hardware, photography equipment, and just about any item one needed to make repairs around the house or farm. Photo courtesy of Delaware Public Archives.

---

4. My first recollection of going off the peninsula was a Cub Scout trip to see the Baltimore Orioles when I was eight years old. When I saw the slight hills west of the bay, I thought I was in the mountains.

Joseph's was one of many local dairies that delivered milk in the area. Joseph's delivered to our home. Mom set the empty bottles on our step and they were replaced the next morning. Photo by the author.

Our neighbors had home delivery of Bond Bread for all their bread and pastries.

Except for our trips to Harold Purnell's Hardware Store to pick up needed hardware, this was the only trip to town by the males.

Mom went to town once a week on Thursdays. There were no large shopping centers or malls. Most of the stores, except the small country stores, were in the downtown area of the towns. While in town, Mom did her grocery shopping at the Clover Farm store (more recently the 3 Bears Nursery on North Bedford Street), got her hair done, and bought an early Sunday edition of the *New York Daily News*. My sister and I eagerly awaited the bag of penny candy Mrs. Rogers always gave Mom for us kids.

In later years, Mom shopped at the Acme on East Market Street, which gave S&H Green stamps based on the amount of the purchase. We normally saved them in old shoe boxes until we were ready to redeem them. We then spent an evening placing the stamps in books which we took to the S&H redemption store in Dover. Later, one opened on East Market Street next to the Acme Market in Georgetown. When I went into Weblos (a branch of Scouting between Cub Scouts and Boy Scouts), we used the stamps for the camping supplies.

Even though we lived in the country and were somewhat isolated, we had more home deliveries than now. We had deliveries/salesmen from Stanley Products, TV repairmen, doctor visits (when we were sick), Joseph's Dairy (we left empty milk bottles on

S&H Green Stamps were given with purchases at the Acme Markets which many still referred to as The American Store, its predecessor. The stamps were placed in the booklet for redeemption.

Rural Life in the 1950's and 60's

the step that were replaced by full bottles), dry cleaners, fish salesmen in season; and our neighbors even had bread delivered by the Bond Bread man.

The Tastee Freeze was the first fast food establishment in our area. We often went to the Tastee Freeze after church on Sundays, for their special deal of five hamburgers for a dollar.

Nearly everyone in the neighborhood was involved with agriculture in some fashion. Some had other jobs to supplement their farm income, and others may have simply rented their land, but farming was in their blood and part of their roots.

For farm families, weekdays and Saturdays were no different unless you were of school age. Farming was not a nine to five, five-day-a-week job. Saturday was another workday.

Sundays, however, were special days. We were taught to "remember the Sabbath and to keep it Holy." That meant no work except what was required to tend to livestock. It was a day of worship, relaxation, and being with family. Mom prohibited us from playing any card games, from sewing, or even using scissors on Sundays. This did not seem unusual to us because everyone in our circle of friends and neighbors did the same.

The day started with Church as is detailed later. After Church, we often took rides and viewed the crops, took special trips to museums, and sometimes went to view the "Sycamore Store."

Often, Dad walked the back fields with us in search of arrowheads and other Indian artifacts. We walked between the corn or soybean rows, looking for artifacts on the bare ground. It was usually most productive after a rain, which tended to wash the dirt off the artifacts, making them easier to find. We found arrowheads, axes, mortars, knives, and large amounts of pottery. Our trips to local museums often involved comparing what we found on the farm to the museum collection.

Sunday afternoons were often spent walking the fields looking for arrow heads and other Native American artifacts. Photo by the author.

Other times, Sunday rides ended at the Tastee Freeze, the first fast food place we knew of, and got five hamburgers for $1.00. There were no shopping trips, because stores were closed on Sundays. In fact, Maryland had Blue Laws, which prohibited them from being open.[5]

The Sycamore store now sits in the side yard at home. My father commented that his parents would meet in the store. It sat next to the farm where my great-grandfather was once a tenant farmer. My father had it moved from Sycamore to our farm and was restoring it for use as our church museum when he died. Photo by the author.

---

5 The Blue Laws were so named in 1781 by the Reverend Samuel Peters when he used that term to refer to the laws that the Puritans in New England states enacted to control morality. In 1961 the US Supreme Court upheld the constitutionality of the laws. These laws are primarily seen in regards to alcohol sales today.

Rural Life in the 1950's and 60's

Georgetown Little League

This is the Bluerocks Little League Team, which was one of four teams in the Georgetown League in the late 1950's. The players on the back row from left to right: Steve White, Johnny Gorlich, Mark Workman, Rick Dodd, David Collins, Bobby Martin; bottom row left to right: Billy Reed Hudson, Vic Greenwalt, Wayne Carey, Linden Mitchell, the 8 year old author, and Buddy Watson. Photo from the author's collection.

Recreation

Although we had TV, it did not play a large part in our lives. We worked and played outside. There were no computers and no interactive games. After school I immediately headed outdoors. I was often occupied by simply throwing the ball in the air to catch or throwing a rubber ball or tennis ball against the barn. I spent a lot of time climbing—it might be trees, up the loft, or even up a roof. There was a catalpa tree[1] behind the house that was perfect for climbing. Dad had also planted sycamore trees in the yard that were easy to climb to the top. Mom, who was afraid of heights and afraid I might fall, often summoned Merrill to get me down. He was always unsympathetic to my plight and responded that since I got up there myself I could get down myself.

I often got together to play baseball with friends and relatives in the neighborhood. These were not organized games. We called to see who was available and then rode our bikes to the agreed meeting place to play. If there was only one or two available, we settled for "pitch and catch" or "pops and rollers."

There were never enough people to have two entire teams. Usually the players consisted of my cousin, Lynn Moore, the Connor boys (James, Charles, Ronnie and Jackie), and sometimes Rodney Wilson. Billy G. Rust would also sometimes play.

When the older boys played, it was my brother Merrill, Wayne Rust, Jimmie Truitt, Jr., Nelson Justice, Joe (Sonny) Holson, the Wilson boys - Richard, Ronald, Robert, James, and Kenny.

Usually there were two or three bats in the neighborhood, two or three balls and several mitts or gloves. Everyone brought what they had and we shared. I never had a new glove. I always used a hand-me-down glove from

---

1. That is the tree that lines the streets in front of the Governor's Mansion in Williamsburg, Virginia. It has large leaves and long banana like seed pods.

my brother, Merrill. That was the norm in the neighborhood.

The baseballs we used were rarely new and often did not have the original covers. We used baseballs so much that the covers eventually came off. Out came the "black tape" to the rescue. This tape was not the black plastic electrical tape of today. It was actually a sticky tape many referred to as "tar tape." This had many uses besides as a replacement cover on baseballs (always referred to as "hardballs"). If we broke our bat, we simply taped up the handle and continued to use it. We didn't trash it and buy a new bat. [2]

In the summer I also collected and traded baseball cards. These were usually purchased at the Little League park and came five to a pack with bubble gum enclosed. At that time (before free agency), players often stayed with a team their entire careers. Some popular baseball cards in 1962: Stan Musial, Hank Aaron, Warren Spahn, Micky Mantle, and Brooks Robinson. Photo by the author, courtesy of Jamie Sharp.

The games might take place in a field, pasture or side yard. The older boys also played on the Church team which Uncle Carlton organized. That was the only organized team in the neighborhood.

Another important activity was attending and participating in school sports events. My brother, Merrill, played both football and baseball and we attended all his games. He played Pony League baseball in the summer and school ball during the school year. When he played, there was no Little League in the area. I did participate in Little League. The fields were located where the Possum Point Players' building is now.

Living in a sparsely populated area our bikes were an important mode of transportation. They were the basic single speed bikes with a coaster brake. I never owned a bike with multiple speeds.[3]

A typical bike or "two wheeler" of the time with a coaster brake. Often we added lights, even though we rarely rode at night, and a basket to carry baseball mitts or discarded soft drink bottles we found for redemtion at the store.

---

2. Our bats were wood, usually made from ash. Louisville Sluggers were the top of the line bats. No one heard of bats made from aluminum or composites.
3. Merrill did get an "English" bike one year that had three speeds. It had narrow tires and was not really suited for use in the country. It was hard to ride on the dirt roads.

Rural Life in the 1950's and 60's

Often, I just jumped on my bike and took a ride with no specific destination in mind. Traffic was extremely light—many times I could ride to Wilson's Store without seeing a single car. In fact, I would often ride to the store without using my hands on the handlebars.

Every kid knew how to do basic bicycle repairs. We released the air in the tire to fix a pinched valve stem, straightened it, and pumped it back up. If we had a hole in the tube we removed the tire, made the patch and remounted the tire and were back in action. Likewise, we knew how to put a chain back on if it slipped off and how to tighten the chain. To make a bike sound like a motorcycle, kids taped baseball cards to the front fork positioned to hit the spokes. Others put raccoon tails in the ends of the rubber hand grips. If the hand grips came off, "black" or "tar" tape came to the rescue and we taped the hand grips. We did not take the bike to a repair shop. I don't even know if one existed, nor did we wait for an adult to fix these minor matters.

Roller skates were strapped to one's shoes and tightened with a key. They had steel wheels and were used on rough surfaces. Photo by the author.

Times that we got together with friends to play were treats. This usually only happened in the summer, and only after we finished our chores. Other games we played when we got

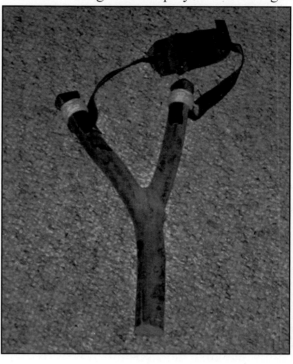

While cleaning the house after Mom's death, I not only found that she had saved my first Little League uniform and my Cub Scout uniform, but also this slingshot I made. Photo by the author.

together, in addition to baseball and football, were tag, hide-and-go-seek, or war. Some of my friends had pogo sticks and skates (the kind that attached to the bottom of the shoe with a key), but they were impractical in the country without extensive sidewalks. Likewise, basketball was not a big sport with country kids. Most had a hoop on the side of a barn to play "Horse" or other shooting games, but dribbling was difficult without paved surfaces. We did have some sidewalks at our home which was great for my sister to play hop scotch. We did fall prey to the hula hoop craze, but it only occupied a few minutes of time before it became passe.

In one of the experiments at the airport, Ford pick ups were dropped from the back of planes. Melvin Joseph bought them and refurbished them for use by his construction company. His daughter, Joe Ann Adams, told the author that one of the trucks is still owned by the company. Photo courtesy of Hagley Museum and Library.

Most of the time I just played alone—I was always exploring —the barns, the fields, and the woods. It was not uncommon for me to spend all day outside in the woods and only come in to get something to eat. To help pass the time, I often cut a sapling to make a homemade bow and arrow or slingshot. Unfortunately, either because of my building skills or my marksmanship, my homemade weapons were not very accurate.

The dirt road in front of the house provided entertainment after a rain. The ditches filled with water and my sister and I kept ourselves occupied catching tadpoles, digging clay to make small items, or looking for fossils. Over the years, I found numerous stones with seashell fossils.

In late summer and early fall I ventured into the woods in search of huckleberries. They tended to grow in the areas along the roadways and in the thinner areas of the woods where the sun could hit the forest floor. Although I only picked what I could eat, Mom told of families picking huckleberries for jellies and preserves when she was young. She recalled that they tied cloth soaked in coal oil to keep off chiggers (pronounced "jiggers").[4]

During the summer months, the National Guard camped on the airport grounds all along the area now known as Park Boulevard. When they broke camp and left, we rode our bikes all through the area and retrieved such abandoned treasures as tent stakes, walkie talkie wire, KP rations, etc.

Back then that area was simply known as "the airport." There was no fire school or Industrial Park. It was just an abandoned World War II airport. The only tenant that I recall was All-American Engineering, which operated from what was then, and for many years thereafter, the only large building at the airport. At one time, they made blimps at that location. As noted later in the "Memorable Events" section of this book, the most visible and exciting of their projects was the launch of the rocket sled.

There were other airport activities that amused the neighborhood. Word circulated that they dropped Ford pick-up trucks from the back of airplanes as part of an experiment for the military. Melvin Joseph bought the

---

4. Chiggers are extremely small insects that cause severe itching where they bite. Some claim they burrow into the skin while others state they only bite and leave and the salava causes the itch. I have seen literature stating both. In the south, they are referred to as redbugs.

Rural Life in the 1950's and 60's

trucks for use in his construction company.

They also made a mock-up of an airplane from pipe and metal tubing. We all wondered how it was to be put to use. It was shot from the rocket sled track into some type of webbing. It was later learned that the experiment was to test webbing as a safety device to prevent planes from overshooting a runway.

One activity at the airport created a lot of excitement for all the kids in the neighborhood. Small parachutes were dropped with some kind of devices and small flashlights attached. Rumor was that they were dropped to determine air currents. We rode our bikes on all the field and woods roads in anticipation of finding these prizes.

A more traditional form of rural recreation was shooting. Most kids had BB guns or .22s, referred to as bullet rifles. We often walked the roads, shooting blackbirds off the telephone and electric lines with the BB guns. The bullet rifles were used in target practice to shoot cans as our targets or to shoot the crows that ate the seed from fields.

These are the style of guns owned by many in the rural community. The top is a single shot 410 shotgun given to me by my Grandfather Wilson on my 16th birthday. The bottom gun is a single shot .22 caliber rifle, normally referred to at that time as a "bullet rifle." Photo by the author.

As in the case of sporting goods, guns were often hand-me-down. I always used one of Merrill's or Dad's guns when I went hunting. The first gun I bought was a 22 caliber rifle and then I received a Harrington & Richardson 410 gauge shotgun as a gift from my grandfather Wilson which was suitable for squirrel hunting.

Most hunting in my early years was for squirrel. I hunted some with Dad, although he rarely hunted. We sat and watched the oak trees for squirrels jumping from tree to tree. Consequently, one needed a calm day to notice the movement in the trees. As a young active child that was too sedentary.

When I got older, my brother, Merrill, took me walking around corn fields to squirrel hunt. We walked quietly, and we could actually hear the squirrels gnawing on the corn. As we approached, they ran back to the woods. They often climbed the nearest tree and stopped approximately waist high, and we then shot them. After the hunt, we took the squirrels to Helen Truitt and usually stayed and helped her clean them. They were a welcome treat to her.

Delaware did not have a deer season until 1954, and it was only three days long. It was rare to see a deer. In fact, when Jimmie Truitt, Jr. killed a deer, it was such big news that it was on the front page of the *Sussex Countian*. Deer hunting was not high-tech at all. We used the same guns we used for other hunting but shot either a "pumpkin ball" or buckshot. The guns were not very accurate.

They were smooth bore, not the rifled barrels in use today, and normally did not have sights and definitely did not have scopes. The only deer stands were ones people built out of wood. It seemed it was always cold, and we did not have the pocket hand warmers, toe warmers, Gore Tex or Thinsulate that we have today to keep us dry and warm. When someone killed a deer, it was the common practice to hang it on a tree in the front of the house or somewhere else visible to the road. I have also seen people with a deer tied over the hood and front fender of their car as they drove through town, making sure everyone knew of their successful hunt.

We did not hunt birds, although our property—and in fact the whole neighborhood—was known for its many coveys of quail. Reese Swain, our dentist, and Chief Harold Todd, our town police chief, often hunted quail on our farm. Our friend and neighbor, Jimmie Truitt, Sr., was well known as a quail hunter, and many from town liked to hunt with him because he knew all the good spots.

Rehoboth Beach was not as busy as now. During week days there were fewer sun-bathers than shown in this picture. Other beaches, with even less people, enjoyed by the locals, were Coin Beach and Tower Beach. Photo courtesy of Delaware Public Archives.

Many went to Rehoboth after Church or on Sunday evenings to have french fries, carmel pop-corn, and to visit and chat with friends. Photo courtesy of Delaware Public Archives.

Rabbit hunting was a tradition for many on Thanksgiving morning and the day after Thanksgiving. Merrill did have some beagles (rabbit dogs) but to this day I have never hunted rabbits.

We likewise did not hunt geese or ducks. I did enjoy seeing the migratory geese as they flew south for the winter. The sky seemed covered with the Canada geese in their vee formations. Unfortunately, most of the Canada geese we see today are resident geese and stay here year-round, living near development and golf course ponds. The migratory geese that we do see are snow geese, which were unheard of in this area when I was a boy.

Even though we only lived 12 miles from the ocean, the beach did not play a big part in our lives. We went to Rehoboth only once or twice each summer to play on the beach and swim. However, we did go to the beach in the evenings—usually on Sunday night—to get Dolly's popcorn, buy french fries doused

Rural Life in the 1950's and 60's

in vinegar, and walk the boardwalk. We often saw many in the farm community or our relatives congregating on the boardwalk. One must-visit as kids while in Rehoboth was Funland on the boardwalk. After Labor Day, Rehoboth was boarded up and went into hibernation until Memorial Day weekend.

During the winter school months, all kids dreamed of a snow day. When the rare snowstorm occurred, we built snowmen and snow forts and had the occasional snowball fight. Since there were no hills, we resorted to pulling our sleds behind tractors or cars. Snowstorms actually meant more work than play.[5]

Music went through a major transition during that period. The music went from rock and roll and American Bandstand with Dick Clark, to the British invasion of the 60s and to Flower Power of the late 60s. In the 50s, our record player only played 45 rpm records, and my tape deck was reel to reel. In the late 60s, the eight track tape decks became popular, soon followed by cassette tapes and now CDs. The Beatles influenced everything from their first appearance on the Ed Sullivan Show in 1964 to the present day. Haircuts went from a tapered cut—combed back with hair tonic—to a combed forward over the forehead style.

There was a movie theater in town, Ayers' Theater. I rarely went...I probably only saw two or three movies prior to seventh grade. There was no rating system for movies.... everything was family fare. The James Bond movies were the first risque' movies, and they were tame by today's standards.

When I went to the movies, it seemed that everyone hung out at Henry's Newstand both before and after the movies. There was a lunch counter, magazines and books, and a pinball machine that always had a line of people waiting to play (to reserve one's spot, one placed their nickle on the top of the machine). Henry's also had a juke box.

The juke box was a popular item in Henry's. All the kids played their favorite tunes while waiting for the movies or while hanging out after the movies. All diners, truck stops, newstands and hangouts had a juke box. Many also had table top versions at each booth. Photo by the author.

---

5. We became very isolated in snowstorms. Many of the roads were unpaved and were difficult to travel. During one storm when I was in elementary school the National Guard used tanks to get supplies to the outlying areas. Another memorable snowstorm occurred in 1967. We had an exchange student from Lima, Peru, who had never seen snow. I was awakened as he ran from window to window to watch the snow. We had to help Dad all day in the chicken houses knocking the drifts from the back of the houses. Jose did not want to see more snow.

After I got my license, I usually went to theaters in other towns. There was the Layton Theater in Seaford, Midway Theater between Rehoboth and Lewes, (which at the time only had one theater), Blue Hen Theater in Rehoboth, where Carlton's Men's Store is today, Clayton Theater in Dagsboro, and several theaters in Salisbury, Maryland.

There was also a drive-in theater in Midway but I only went one time. The window had to be left down to allow the speaker to be placed in the car through the side window It was hot in the summertime, and bugs and mosquitoes swarmed in the car. Going to the drive -in was already passe by the time I got my license, and most theaters had closed or were soon to close.

Rural Life in the 1950's and 60's

The Office

The Moore Brothers office and warehouse were located at what is now known as the northeast corner of Springfield Road and Park Avenue, east of Georgetown, Delaware. The building to the left was the original building and in my youth was primarily used for storage. It originally housed the local Southern States franchise. The building to the right served as both warehouse and office building. In the tradition of the area that building had been moved approximately one mile to this location. Sketch by Carlton R. Moore.

Moore Brothers

Moore Brothers was for many years one of the top two or three wholesale distributors of poultry and animal pharmaceuticals on Delmarva. It started out as a local feedstore, owned by Uncle Charles and Dad. They did not manufacture their own feed but distributed feed made by others. This business had its roots in my grandfather's early success in the chicken business.

My grandfather was an entrepreneur who owned and operated businesses in Georgetown.[1] He owned and operated an incubator at home for hatching eggs After they were hatched, my grandfather raised the chickens until they were 2 3/4 to 3 1/2 pounds. Many of the neighbors came and helped him slaughter, clean, pack, and ice down chickens on Friday mornings. This was done early enough in the morning so that he was able to arrive in Rehoboth Beach before noon. He then went to the local hotels and restaurants and sold the chickens and took orders for the next week. He did this from the 1920s until the early 1930s. Although he quit "huckstering" chickens at that time, he still had the incubators and either grew chickens for himself or hatched for friends and neighbors.

MOORE BROS.
Wholesale Distributors
PHARMACEUTICALS - BIOLOGICALS
ANTI-BIOTICS - OILS
SULFAS - VACCINES
GEORGETOWN, DELAWARE
PHONES: { Office 2085
Residence 6874, 2871, 6947
If You Need Something in a Hurry Call Us
NITE OR DAY
WE DELIVER — Small or Large Orders
Always Call COLLECT

This was the letterhead for the company listing the products sold. Please note that the only address needed was Georgetown without route number or box number. Also note the four digit phone numbers. From the author's collection.

---

1. He owned a tobacco and candy store in Georgetown and also owned the Georgetown Marble and Granite Works which sold and engraved tombstones. He owned the marble yard business with his father in law Ed Russell. In later years it was operated by George Russell, my great uncle, and was located on the northeast corner of Pine and South Bedford Street. They also had an auxiliary location in Salisbury, Maryland. My grandfather also had a gas pump and sold gas at home.

After his success with incubators, it was a natural progression for the family to get more involved in this new industry.

When Uncle Charles returned home from the war, he and Dad developed the business plan for what was to become Moore Brothers. Based on my grandfather's experience with chickens, they saw the need for a regional distributor of feed, medicines, and vaccines. The medicines and vaccines later became

The antibiotic, Terramycin, was probably the best known poultry medication at the time. It was used to treat coccidiosis, a prevalent disease in chickens. Photo by the author courtesy of the Delaware Agricultural Musem and Village.

the main focus of the company. Uncle Charles wrote letters to the feed and vaccine companies and obtained the franchise rights to sell their products.

They bought the land and original building for their operation from Francis Truitt, who operated a Southern States franchise[2] just down the road from the Moore family where Springfield Road now dead-ends at Park Boulevard. It was located on the northeast corner, now the site of a private residence.

Moore Brothers sold vaccines, pharmaceuticals, and medicines in bulk to local feed stores. At times local farmes bought feeds and medicines for use on their farms. Scales such as these were used in the repackaging process for these individual sales. Photo by the author courtesy of the Delaware "Agricultural Musem and Village.

---

2. Francis Truitt was married to Helen Truitt, nee Walls, and they were the ones who converted Springfield School #33 to a store, Truitt's Store, now known as Wilson's Store.

Rural Life in the 1950's and 60's

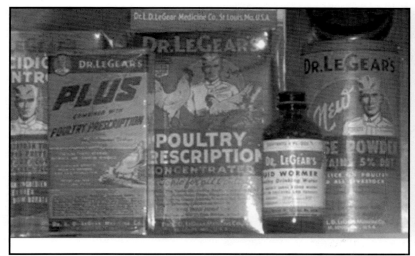

Many of the earlier vaccines and supplements were marketed as if they were prescribed medicines. Note the use of the word "prescription" in the products shown above. Many "Emulsions" were sold for various poultry cures. Photo courtesy of Delaware Agricultural Museum and Village.

There were two buildings—one was a narrow building with an office in front and a warehouse area in the rear, which was located the closest to Park Avenue, and the other was a newer, one-story building that was wide and built in a style similar to many of the feed houses that dotted the peninsula. The newer building housed the office during my childhood.

During this time of great change, the Delmarva Peninsula was dotted with similar feed houses. It was a time when farmers and growers were no longer willing to accept the burden and risk of growing chickens on their own. Like other feed houses at the time—including the big companies now— Moore Brothers had people growing chickens for them on contract. At that time, the arrangement was similar to share cropping. The farmers received two-thirds of the profits for use of their chicken houses and labor, and Moore Brothers received one-third for providing the chicks, feed, litter, and medication. These feed dealers bought their chicks, their feed, and medicines from independent wholesale suppliers. They rarely bought all from the same company. Moore Brothers sold the medicines to those other feedhouses.

My grandfather was the salesperson who traveled the peninsula to visit their 225 distributors (other feedhouses) throughout Delaware and the eastern shore of Maryland and Virginia. His past experience selling chickens and his entrepreneurial background proved to be a welcome asset. At that time, individual contacts were crucial. There were no fax machines to take orders, and no web sites or e-mails. Although phones were important for taking the orders, the initial contact and trust was built on a one-on-one and face-to-face basis. In later years, I remember him spending time in the office, smoking his pipe and either working on crossword puzzles or writing religious poetry.[3]

---
3. See Appendix 2 for some of his poetry.

My father handled the deliveries. The office was close enough that Dad would often stop at home before going on a delivery. I took many preschool trips with Dad as he delivered medicines and vaccines to the feed houses around the peninsula. There

In the early days of the poultry industry, there were many miricale addiitives and medicines marketed for both rapid growth and as cures for diseases. Photo courtesy of Delaware Agricultural Museum and Village.

were times that Mom would go to the office to answer the phone if everyone else was tied up, but that was a rare occasion. Other times, I went to the office to spend time with PopPop, Uncle Charles, and Dad.

The poultry industry changed significantly in the early 1950s. At that time, large companies (referred to as "integrators")[4] dominated the industry. Some of the first integrators were Perdue, Townsends, Workman Brothers, Wilsons, and Allens. Most growers now grow for one of the large integrators such as Tyson, Mountaire, Allens, or Perdue. The growers did not buy their own chicks, feed, and medicines. In fact, they didn't own the chicks. The integrator provided those items and the grower provided the housing, electricity and other utilities and the labor. The integrator then paid the grower, based on a complex feed conversion formula (calculated on the amount of feed required to convert into a pound of chicken with the costs factored in) as set forth in their contract. There was normally a guaranteed minimum per thousand and then a bonus system based on performance. That system is still in use today.

Because of the change in the market, which found the number of feed stores reduced from 225 to less than a dozen, Dad

This was an old style adding machine similar to one used at the office. They also has a newer model and allowed me to play with this one. After punching the numbers a handle was pulled to register them. Photo by the author courtesy of Delaware Agriculture Museum and Village.

and Uncle Charles acquired farm and timber land while de-emphasizing their reliance on the poultry industry. They formally ceased operations in the 1960s.

---

4. They were referred to as integrators because they provided vertical integration from the hatching of the chicks to the processing of the meat and every stage in between.

Rural Life in the 1950's and 60's

Work /Chores

The author on the Case 800 with his nephew, Eric, on his lap. The Farmall H is shown behind them.

Work /Chores

We always had chores to do around home. We took turns helping Mom with the dishes. Usually one of us washed and the other dried. There were no dish washers at the time. Likewise, no one had, or had even heard of, electric or gas clothes driers at that time. Everyone had a clothes line from tree to tree or post to post. We helped Mom hang clothes on the clothes line and helped bring in the clothes when they were dry.

Mom always ironed our clothes. This was before the days of permanent press or wash and wear. It was important to Mom that we looked our best. Even though steam irons were just becoming available, they used distilled water and Mom continued to iron as she always had. She usually had a pan of water nearby, and she dipped her hand in the water and "sprinkled" the clothes as she ironed. Many others used empty ketchup or similar shaped bottles with holes punched into the lid similar to a salt-shaker top. The bottle was filled with water and the clothes were sprinkled while ironing.

When Mom cleaned the house, we often were asked to take the rugs out to the clothesline to "beat" them. Although there

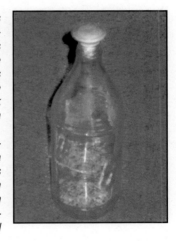

Many used bottles such as this to "sprinkle" water on clothes while ironing. There were many variations of this type of bottle but this one has a cork stopper attached to a metal top with holes. Mom preferred to simply dip her hand in a pot of water for this chore. Even though we gave her a steam iron it was years before she actually used it. Part of the reason was habit and the other reason was it, at that time, required distilled water. Mom would not waste money to buy distilled water when her tried and true method was free. Photo by the author.

was a tool or device specifically for rug beating, we usually hung the rugs on the line and then hit or "beat" the rugs with a broom to clean them.

Ronald was then, as now, an entrepreneur. He thought that there was money in bees and bought some hives. I remember his bee suit and smoker. He came in one day and even with his suit he was stung multiple times. That effectively ended his bee keeping.

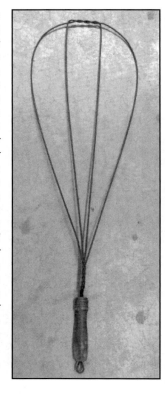

The item to the right is a rug beater. It was used to beat the dirt out of rugs. The rugs were taken to the clothes line, draped over the line and then hit with the "beater" until all the dirt was removed. We did have a rug beater similar to this however Mom normally sent us outside to do this job with the broom. She had us lay the rugs on the sidewalk and sweep all the dirt off first and then hang them over the line and use the broom to beat the dirt. The broom was heavier and the longer handle gave more leverage allowing us to beat the rugs harder. Photo by the author.

Mom and Dad were apparently very supportive of his entrepreneurial streak, because later he decided that raising hogs was the way to riches. To my knowledge, we had not raised hogs before, and physical changes were made to the barn. The former cattle pound area was converted for hogs, and the stalls in the barn were set up for birthing of pigs.

When I was in the third grade, Dad nailed boards to the corners of the stalls and set up heat lamps in those areas. Those were areas where the piglets could get warm, and the boards prevented the piglets from being squashed by the sow. It was not uncommon for a sow to lay down and actually kill young pigs by laying on them. When the pigs were being born, Dad and I stayed up all night and wiped off the piglets as they were born and placed them under the heat lamp. Depending on whether the sow had given birth before or not, there could be a dozen or more piglets per litter.

We did not butcher the hogs ourselves as many did in Sussex. We sold them at the market. Hog killings were a family tradition for many. Though the work was hard, it was eagerly anticipated. It was an all day event, and the family (often the extended family of aunts, uncles, cousins and friends) made sausage, scrapple, ham, bacon, and lard. Each family had its own special seasoning and recipe. The large cast iron pots often seen today in yards as decorations, looking like witches brew kettles, were hog-killing pots.

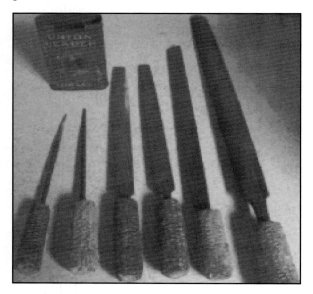

Everything was saved and one made do with what one had. Dad's files needed handles so he used corncobs which were readily available. The Union Leader tobacco tin was used to store his line level. Photo by the author.

Rural Life in the 1950's and 60's

Just as Mom kept us busy inside, Dad always managed to keep us busy with chores outside. Everybody was thrifty and recycled. When something was broken, it was fixed with whatever material was at hand. It was not thrown away. If one needed handles on files, one used corn cobs. When buildings or structures were demolished, all the materials were saved for reuse - EVEN THE BENT NAILS. On more than one occasion, Merrill and I sat on a concrete block, using a hammer to straighten a bucket of nails that Dad had pulled out. Likewise, all bricks and blocks were recycled. We often spent time with a hammer, knocking off the old mortar so they could be reused.

One summer Dad was concerned with the amount of weeds in our 35-acre soybean field. He was afraid the weeds would "go to seed" and cause more weeds the following year. Dad sharpened the "fodder"[1] knives and Dad, Merrill and I walked between the rows of soybeans and chopped the tops off weeds even with the tops of the soybeans. I was very young and the tops of the soybeans were about chest high to me. The beans were wet in the morning and we were quickly soaked, but the work and warming sun soon dried us out.

In 1956, when I was six, Dad and Mom bought some farms between Routes 30 and 5, south of Route 9. These farms are located on what is now known as Anderson Corner Road and Doddtown Road. The northeast corner of Doddtown and Anderson Corner Roads was 54 acres of woods. Dad cleared that and created a large, nearly-square field. We always referred to those farms as the "New Ground." In fact, in later years when we placed the tract in an Agricultural Preservation District, we officially named the District the "New Ground District."

Hog killing pots and sheer poles are rarely used today but are often seen as decorations. The pot was hung from the sheer poles over a low fire to render down the lard or mixes for scrapple or sausage. Photo by the author courtesy of Raymond Joseph.

---

1. A knife somewhat like a machete that was used to cut corn stalks for fodder. Prior to the advent of mechanized corn pickers farmers used not only the ears of corn for livestock feed but also the stalks to feed cows and horses. The stalks were stored in the fields by stacking them in shocks that looked like teepees. They looked similar to the Halloween decorations of today.

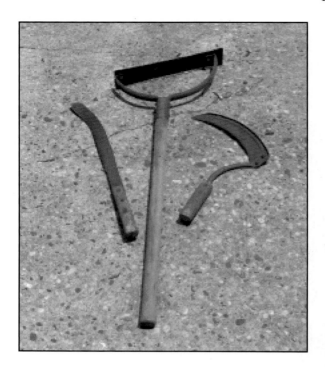

The above tools were the weed eaters of my generation. The tool to the left is a "foddler knife" used to cut corn stalks to be used as fodder (feed) for the animals. We often used it to cut weeds. The tool in the center was referred to as a weed whip or double sided sickle. It was sharp on both sides and was swung back and forth to cut weeds. The tool to the right is a small hand sickle that was used to cut weeds in tight quarters or around posts and buildings. Photo by the author.

One might think that the bulldozers with root rakes would remove all the trunks, limbs and stumps so that the field could be planted. That was not the case. Although today there are machines to pull behind tractors to pick up the remaining sticks, it was not the case in the 50's and 60's. Before anything could be planted, we had to "pick up sticks." Starting in the third grade and for the next three years, my summer job was "picking up sticks." For those uninitiated, picking up sticks is a boring, nasty job. The ground was uneven and in the dry summer was powdery. It was very much like walking on a sandy beach all day. When we threw the sticks on the wagon, dirt and dust blew down our shirts.

At that time, we had a Farmall "A" tractor with a two wheeled wagon. We started at one end of the field and threw sticks and roots into the wagon. When it was loaded, we unloaded it by hand into a pile that was eventually burned. It took from breakfast to lunch to get from one end of the field to the other, and then from lunch to supper to get back to the other end.

This is a Farmall A tractor. This is the type tractor I first learned to drive and the tractor we used in the summers "picking up sticks" in the new ground. It is a small tractor often used to till gardens. Photo by the author.

Even though the job was hot and nasty, Dad did his best to make it fun. He commented on how the piles looked like tepees and would often wonder aloud about how the land looked before the first settlers. To this day, when hunting or just outside on the land, I often wonder what the land looked like 100 or 200 years ago. I was also aware of how much more difficult it was to clear

Rural Life in the 1950's and 60's

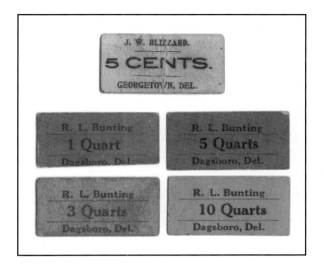

When people picked strawberries for a grower they did not get paid each day. Instead they were given a ticket that had the growers name and the number of quarts picked. At a later date, often when the grower got paid, they would redeem the tickets for cash. From the author's collection.

land a generation or two before my time. I often heard my great aunt and other relatives discuss her husband getting up before light and with "lantern-light" use an axe to clear new ground.

Dad was always interested in purchasing more land. I often traveled with him as a young boy to look at new tracts. There were many tracts referred to as "cut-over." These were tracts that had the timber cut and consisted of shrubs, young growth, and stumps from the cut trees. This land could be purchased for $50.00 an acre at that time. When the timber was cut, oftentimes a saw mill was actually set up on the site to do all the cutting into logs.

During that same time period, Dad planted approximately a half acre of strawberries in the field in front of the house. We kept busy hoeing and weeding the patch. We sold "U Pick" strawberries for 25 cents per quart.

This was exciting to my sister and me, as many "town folks," often our teachers, came to the house to pick strawberries.

Although our patch was larger than most, nearly everyone had a strawberry patch. Our area, and a large part of the county and peninsula, had been known for its strawberries that were shipped to the markets in the cities. Basil Perry was the most prominent strawberry grower and shipper in our neighborhood. Basil not only shipped berries but also was a large shipper of plants for transplanting.

John Blizzard, who lived on Route 30 between St. John's Church and Zoar Church, was another. I recently came across a strawberry ticket from his operation.

These are chicken coops. They are used to transport chickens. The buildings they live in are chicken houses; not coops, per Sussex parlance. Photo by the author courtesy of the Delaware Agricultural Museum and Village.

When I entered Seventh Grade, Dad decided to go back into the chicken business. He found two chicken houses[2] for sale in Milton. Dad employed a house mover,

Throughout this book there are references to buildings being moved from one location to another, e.g., the old Church, chicken houses, the Sycamore store. Above is the law office of Everett Warrington being moved in Georgetown. Photo courtesy of Delaware Public Archives.

Charlie O'Day of Redden, who braced the houses and cut them into movable sections. Each house was 455 feet long and 16 feet wide. Once cut, they would fall apart unless 2" x 6" cross bracing was properly in place. The pieces were jacked up, placed on a truck and moved to our farm. The pieces were then placed on a new foundation, and we had to reconnect the pieces. This was my job during the summer between Seventh and Eighth Grades.[3]

One of the main jobs I had was roof repair. The roofs were cedar shingle and chain saws were used to cut the houses. I took off the shingles back a foot or so from the cut and then replaced those shingles. One tool I used looked like a bar used to open cars that has the keys locked in. With a hammer, I drove it under the shingles and around the nails. Then I hit it with a hammer to cut the nail and pull out the shingle. I also used a shingle hatchet to cut the wood shingles to the exact size.

We also installed the plumbing. There were no plastic pipes at that time, all pipes were galvanized. The pipe was bought in large quantities without threads. The pipes were cut to length, and then they were inserted in a pipe vise for purposes of putting the threads on the ends of the pipe. We installed over 1100 linear feet, plus enough

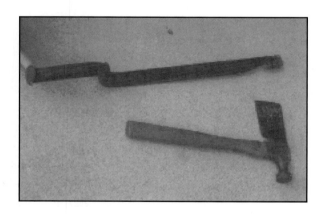

These were the tools I used much of the summer between my 7th and 8th grades. The top tool slipped between shingles and hooked the shingle nails with the notched cutter. A tap by the shingle hatchet shown cut the nail so the defective shingle could be removed. The shingle hatchet was used to split shingles to size and also to nail them in place. Photo by the author.

---

2. Many people new to the area refer to the "houses" as "coops". We consider "coops" to be the small cages that chicken catchers use to transport the chickens from the houses to the processing plant or a small house for 25 to 50 layers. Many use the old wooden coops as Americana decorative pieces.
3. Moving buildings was not uncommon in our history. We did not have portable buildings and as people recycled everthing. . .including buildings. As noted elsewhere, Wilson's Store was moved several times. The original St. John's Church was moved to the home of William (Will) Wilson, later the home of Marshall Wilson of Wilson's Store fame, to be used as a barn. Numerous outbuildings on the Jimmie Truitt farm were moved from other farms, and one of the Moore Brothers buildings was moved to its site from approximately a mile away. There were few, if any, utility lines to impede the moves.

additional piping to connect the houses and all the fixtures.

After the reconstruction of the houses at the new location, we had to get ready for a flock of chickens. We went through an intense preparation period. Since this process was

Manure spreaders at the time were mostly ground driven meaning the turning of the wheel turned all the chains and beaters to operate the spreader. Today most spreaders are PTO (power take off) driven. The spreader was parked in front of a chicken house door and manure was manually loaded in the spreader which was then pulled to the field and spread. Photo by the author.

repeated between every flock and not just for our first flock, my narrative is based on the between flock preparation.

First, we cleaned out manure from the previous flock. It was determined that the biddies[4] obtained immunity by pecking in the litter of the previous flock, so we only cleaned out the wet or crusty areas. Just a few years prior, the custom was to clean out all the litter between every flock. Scoop shovels and manure forks were used. It was impossible not to get some dirt. Therefore, it was often necessary to replace dirt. Piles of fill dirt were dumped in the doors of the chicken house. The dirt was then spread by hand and shoveled in the areas needed.

After the dirt was spread, the sawdust used for litter was dumped in the doors. The sawdust was light and was spread by scoop shovels. This was spread to a 3" or 4" thickness over all the dirt. Cleaning out the houses, shoveling the dirt, and spreading the litter was usually handled by neighborhood teens. Dad normally worked with us. I remember one year a friend from the high school football team came to help to earn some extra money. He had never done this type of work. At one break he came to me and said, "your old man is about to kill me." He further commented that he thought he was in good shape, but no way could he work as hard as Dad.

After the dirt and the sawdust were spread, the gas brooder stoves were then

This is a shed style chicken house popular in the 1950's. The area with the raised roof was the feed room for storage of feed which was delivered in 100 pound bags. Photo by the author.

cleaned and made sure they were in proper working order.[5] We then placed paper under the stoves for the biddies and cleaned and filled the crocks for young chicks. The gallon crocks, often used nowadays as decoration or as lamp bases, were used to provide water.

---

4. Young chickens were referred to as "biddies".
5. When my older brothers were young the houses were heated by coal stoves. The stoves had to be shook down, the ash removed and usually taken to fill holes in the driveway and then new coal put in the stoves. I do barely remember the coal bins and the coal shuttles (buckets) to carry the coal.

These biddies were just a few days old. They are shown under the gas "brooder" stove and eating feed from box lids and drinking from crocks.

They were turned upside down to fill, the plate was then placed over the bottom and then flipped. Some water always came out and soaked the one doing this job.

The day before the biddies were delivered, the gas stoves would be turned on and the

This is the type chicken house that was the norm in the 1950s. This one has a house/apartment on top over the feed room for the tenant that tended the chickens. Those houses/apartments were rarely used by the end of the 1950s. Photo courtesy of Delaware Public Archives.

houses heated to 90+ degrees. The biddies were delivered from the hatchery on the day of their birth. They were delivered in boxes by trucks or converted school buses. Since it was important to get them under the heat as soon as possible, Dad and I helped the delivery man unload and empty the boxes under the stoves. We then set the box tops around the stoves and sprinkled feed in them.

During the summers, weekends, and holidays I helped "tend" the chickens. We had three chicken houses that housed a total of 42,500 chickens. We raised four to five

Chicken crocks were used to water young chicks referred to as "biddies". The plate and the jug were 2 separate pieces and the jug was filled with water, the plate placed on top, and then flipped and put on the ground. By the time enough of these 1 gallon jugs were filled to water 42,500 biddies I was usually soaked. They are often seen around the Peninsula today as americana decorative pieces. Photo by the author.

flocks per year, with each flock staying from nine to ten weeks before going to market. My chores depended on the age of the chickens.

During the first week, the care was intense. The crocks had to be filled daily with water as were the box lids with feed. The heat had to be closely monitored. The heat could be 90 degrees in the house and below freezing outside. Moving from one house to the next would require moving from 90 plus degree temperature out to below freezing and then back to 90 plus degrees in a matter of minutes.

Rural Life in the 1950's and 60's

After a week or so, we fell into the routine of feeding every other day, washing out drinkers (the crocks were replaced with hanging drinkers that automatically refilled) with a household broom, and picking up the dead.

We tried to keep the mortality low. Therefore, medicines were routinely mixed in the feed, which was delivered premixed, or were added to the water supply. The names of the diseases reminded one that Delaware was ground zero in production of poultry. The diseases had such names as "New Castle" or "Gumboro." We did not initially have automatic feeders. We had feed bins at the end of each house from which we could fill the feed cart. The cart was on a metal rail, and I pushed it to each "room" and filled the feeders. The feeders each held 25 lbs of

This is a tube style feed scoop like I used. One scoop from the feed cart filled the hanging feeder shown in the next frame. Photo by the author courtesy of Clark White.

feed. I was fortunate because not many years before, feed was delivered to and stored in feed rooms in the chicken houses in 100 lb bags. There was normally one feed room per chicken house.

The two houses we moved from next to the Odd Fellows Cemetery in Milton had feed rooms, and one had a house on top of the feed room for the caretaker to live in. Dad had the house removed from the top of the feed room and had it placed beside the houses in the event he ever needed help with the chickens. After we sold the poultry operation, that same house became the home to two successive families.[6]

This is a hanging feeder like the ones we used in our chicken houses. Each held 25lbs of feed and were adjusted up as the chickens got older which kept the sawdust and litter out of the feed.. Photo by the author courtesy of Clark White.

---

6. There is a great article in the Fall-Winter 1993-94 issue of *Delaware History* written by Kimberly R Sebold, entitled Chicken-House Apartments on the Delmarva Peninsula that describes this practice and includes pictures.

When the chickens were older, we fed them daily. When the chicks lost their down coats and filled in with feathers, the air became thick with dust, small bits of feathers and other particulates one could see. As a teenager, it seemed the mental part of thinking about going to work in the chicken house was harder than the "just doing it." This was especially true in the summer, when

This is a Case 800 tractor. It has a wide front end, meaning the wheels are spaced apart like an automobile as opposed to a tricyle front end. It pulled four plows which were hooked in tandem as shown elsewhere in this chapter.

the particulates were very intense in the heat and humidity. As I sweated, the bits of feathers, feed, and dust stuck to my body. I always worked as fast as possible to get out of the chicken houses and onto a tractor.

Moving day, which was the day that the chickens were taken to market, was eagerly anticipated. Crews of chicken catchers came to the farm usually late at night and worked all night catching and hauling chickens. We had to prepare the houses by moving the feeders and drinkers out of the way of the catchers. They removed the light bulbs in the rooms where they worked in order to calm the chickens. Each catcher passed two handfuls of chickens to the loaders. Each catcher usually had four or five chickens per hand. The loaders then put them in coops on the trucks and took them to the processing plant.

During this same time period, we did traditional farming of corn and soybeans. We had a Case 800 tractor that pulled a four-bottom plow, a WD45 Allis Chalmers Tractor that pulled a three-bottom plow and a Farmall H Tractor that we used for utility purposes.

Both the Case and the Allis Chalmers had wide front ends, and the Farmall had tricycle style front. The wide front ends tended not to get stuck as easy, but the tricycle fronts allowed for almost zero radius turning.

I really enjoyed the plowing. It took several days but was not boring at all. One could observe one's progress, and to help pass the time, I often looked for arrowheads while

This is a WD 45 Allis Chalmers Tractor. It pulled a 3 bottom moldboard plow and was very powerful for its size. It was equipped with both a foot clutch and a hand clutch. My legs were not long enough to reach the foot clutch, so I drove using the hand clutch until I got older. Photo by the author.

plowing. The promise of spring, the smell of the freshly turned soil and the constant, even drone of the tractors made for a pleasant and memorable experience. We started in the morning by gassing up and greasing all equipment. Although we were on different tractors, this was something else that Dad and I did together.

After the fields were plowed, we then disked. We only had one disk, but it was wider than the plows so one person could disk faster than two could plow. I enjoyed it also, but not as much as plowing. Disking was very dusty. The ground was already worked up from plowing, and the rapid speed of disking enveloped the tractor in a cloud of dust. After disking was complete, Dad planted. We had a four-row corn planter, meaning we could plant four rows at once. Just a few years before, everyone had two-row planters. This meant that it would take approximately half the time and fuel expense to plant a field with a four-row planter than with a two-row planter. We planted the corn in 36-inch rows, meaning there were 36 inches between the rows. My father often talked of having planted the corn in hills four feet apart in each direction when he was a young man. The corn was then cultivated in both directions (crosswise and lengthwise).

This is a set of 3 bottom, pull type plows. They are distinguished from three-point hitch or semi-mounted plows because they have three wheels for transport. The 3 bottom refers to the number of plows....in this case three. When one discussed tractors, one normally did not discuss horsepower to describe the power, but how many plows it pulled. Photo by the author.

The disk above is a transport disk similar to the one we used. It was 10 feet wide and could be transported on the road with the wheels. A hydraulic cylinder was connected to the tractor that lifted the disk for transport or dropped it for use in the field. The disk at the bottom is a three-point hitch disk that is hooked to the tractor and is lifted for transport. At the time, Ford and Massey Fergueson tractors used three-point hitch. It is the norm today.. Photos by the author.

At that time, all farmers cultivated their fields. Although some still used front mounted cultivators, most used four-row rear cultivators. Dad did most of the cultivating and the spraying. Dad was very careful with the chemicals use in spraying and would not allow any of us children to spray. We used 2-4-D for weed control and Atrazine for grass control.

We did not have irrigation and only in the later years of this period was I aware of anyone having it, but no one in the neighborhood had it. We were totally dependent on Mother Nature. I vividly remember literally praying for rain during droughts and being bitterly disappointed when the rain clouds circled to the south. Everyone was sure, however, that it would eventually rain during Fair week.

During the fall harvest season, however, we did not want rain. We were especially concerned with hurricanes and nor'easters. The wind and rain made the corn fall and often it would be too wet to get into the fields to harvest the crop.

My favorite time of the farm year was harvest. We had a two-row corn picker. It was not a corn sheller as is in use today. The corn was picked and stored on the cob. A slant-bottom, gravity corn-wagon was pulled behind the tractor and picker to catch the ears of corn as they were harvested. The wagons were then unloaded, and the corn was put into corn "cribs" by use of an elevator. The corn cribs were traditionally made from oak slats that allowed air to circulate and dry the corn. Therefore, the "cribs" were relatively narrow so that the air could circulate to all the corn... otherwise the corn would heat and then mold.

A 2 row mounted cornpicker on a Farmall tractor similar to the one we first owned. The center point was driven between the two corn rows. Chain driven sprockets pulled the corn stalks into the picker and the corn on the cob was separated from the stalk and husk. A corn wagon was pulled behind the picker and the corn. Photo by the author.

This is a 4 row planter. It could be adjusted to plant either corn or soybeans. The tall arms on either side are markers to ensure proper spacing between rows. The round bins or hoppers in the back held the seed and the wheels covered and firmed dirt over the seeds.. It could be adjusted for distance between rows, distance between seed in the row and the depth of seed planting.

This is a New Idea 2 row pull behind cornpicker. This style allowed the farmer on the tractor to be in front of and away from the dust and noise of the machine, unlike the mounted picker previously shown.

Rural Life in the 1950's and 60's

This is a funnel corn wagon. It was towed behind the corn picker and filled, while moving, with the corn. It was then unloaded by use of gravity....and help by farm kids standing on top and kicking the corn.... into a grain elevator which lifted the corn into the cribs. Howard Betts of Stockley, Delaware was credited as having invented the first gravity corn wagon.

During our first year of farming we did not have adequate storage space, so Dad used snow fencing to create rings in which the corn was stored with tarp tops. The next year we built a large corn crib which was basically a pole building with a concrete floor and wire sides.

During this period, Dad and I spent a great deal of time together. During the summers, we started the day together either in the fields or in the chicken house. It also seemed that once a week we took a trek to Mumford's Sheet Metal Works in Selbyville...often it was to buy sheet metal to patch holes in the pickup. It was a trek because Dad had a 1953 Studebaker pick-up that had a top speed of 40 mph. In the winter it was cold because the only heat was from a vent that transferred heat from the engine block. It was amusing the number of times people stopped and inquired about purchasing the truck. Dad always responded in the affirmative but added that the license tag did not go with it. The tag number was C654...in today's market a valuable tag.

This is another ingenious variation of a corncrib located on Route 16 near Milton. It is actually two cribs placed under a single roof. This provided the necessary air circulation as well as providing much needed storage for equipment. Photo by the author with thanks to Chief Mills.

This is a traditional style corncrib on the farm of Richard and Janice Veasey. The slanted sides allowed more air to circulate to dry the corn. Often a lean-to style shed was built on the side to store equipment as was done here. This corn crib was originally on the farm of Basil Perry, approximatley 1/2 mile away. Photo by the author.

There was always work to keep one busy. I cut the grass at the chicken houses with a push mower (two acres or more... believe me, I celebrated when we purchased a Cub Cadet for that chore. Then I washed and stored the crocks when we finished using them, applied burnt motor oil to farm equipment that sat outside, and painted bare wood surfaces with boiled linseed oil. I contend that I have applied more linseed

Dad's license plate from his 1952 Studebaker pickup. Photo by the author.

oil than any person alive. Dad did not paint the chicken house doors, trim and back drop boards. Instead, after we had "laid away" the crops, Dad often had me reapply linseed oil on all the surfaces.[7]

In the winter, we often put equipment in our farm shop to rebuild. Dad rebuilt wagons, manure spreaders, and tractors. One year the Farmall H dropped a cog through the cast iron housing. There was no way to weld the cast iron. The tractor was needed, because we used that tractor for picking corn and utility work. We went to Mumford's for sheet metal and then cut a sheet metal patch. Dad drilled holes in the housing and threaded them for bolts. Then with gasket material he made a patch that held for as long as we owned it.

In 2007, I found a tractor in some brush on a property I had just purchased. Small trees had even grown up through the tractor. I crawled under the tractor and saw that patch, confirming that it was the same Farmall H that Dad repaired. My next big project is the restoration of that tractor.

This is a Farmall H Tractor similar to the one we owned. It had a tricycle front end which gave it a short turning radius. Photo by the author.

---

7. That time period after the crops were planted and the spraying and cultivating was complete.

Rural Life in the 1950's and 60's

St. John's United Methodist Church

The Church sits at the southeast corner of Springfield, Gravel Hill, and Johnson Roads, at an intersection known as Springfield Crossroads. This Church was built in 1907 and was dedicated free of debt in January, 1908. With furnishings and stained glass, the total costs were $4,800.00. Photo by the author.

Church

St. John's United Methodist Church is situated at the intersection of Routes 30 (Gravel Hill Road) and 47 (Springfield Road to the West and Johnson Road to the East) at Springfield Crossroads.[1] The Church is such a predominant feature in the neighborhood that as a child we often received mail addressed simply as "near St. John's."

St. John's was originally established in the 1830's, as Johnson's Society. Their original meetings took place in private homes and then later in Springfield School #33 which is now Wilson's Store, located in the northwest corner of Springfield Crossroads, although it was approximately one-quarter mile west of that location when it served as a school.

The current Church is the second Church at the same approximate location. The first Church, built in 1840, was located within the cemetery wall and is marked by a monument. The current Church was built in 1907 for a total of $4,800.00, which included the stained glass windows and the furnishings.

The large stained glass windows on the west end of the Church. Photo by the author.

---

1. As a child our area was referred to as St. John's. Dad knew historically the crossroads was called Springfield Crossroads. With the help of Leroy Breasure, the State Highway placed a sign with that name. In fact the original tract of land that the Church is situate was named "Springfield".

The Community Hall was originally a Civilian Conservation Corps building from the Great Depression years. During World War II, the CCC camp was converted to a Prisoner-of-War camp. The building was moved to its current location in 1949 and renovated in 1950.

The Church was thus an integral part of our community. In many cases, it was the Church of our parents, grandparents and great-grandparents. It was part of the tradition and way of life of the parishioners.

Our services started with Sunday School at 11:00 a.m. and "preaching," worship service at noon. As part of a Circuit, (the Georgetown Circuit) our worship service was held every other week. St. John's and Zoar had their service one week and Providence and Bethesda the next on a rotating basis year round. Sunday School was held every week.

Sally Truitt (mother of Noah Truitt) was my first Sunday School teacher. When she retired, Mom became the primary age teacher, a position she held for 45 or more years. Consequently she was known as "Aunt Dot" or "Mom Mom Moore" to several generations in the area.

Youth Sunday School classes were held in the Community Hall. After classes were over, we walked to the Church for the closing ceremony. We often arrived before the Adult Sunday School lessons held in the Church were complete. Pop Pop Moore (Larry W. Moore) was the men's teacher and Mom Mom Allie, the women's.

After a short break, our preaching service started, usually without the minister present because he (and in the later years she) needed the drive time after the previous service in one of the other circuit Churches.

The services were not filled with a lot of ritual. There was a responsive reading and a certain song after the collection was taken, but there were no other rituals. The only exceptions I recall were the Sundays that communion was given or when someone-usually a baby- was christened. Services consisted of scripture readings, responsive readings, special singing, congregational singing and the sermon.

Although seats weren't assigned, families tended to sit in the same seats. It always seemed that the entire neighborhood was there. The Church was not air-conditioned at that time, and I remember that people used the fans provided in the book racks to fan themselves.

The Community Hall has been the location of hundreds, if not thousands, of social events for our Church and neighborhood in the last half century. Covered dish dinners, birthday parties, receptions, wakes, Bible School, and the youth Sunday School classes all take place in this hall. Photo by the author.

Rural Life in the 1950's and 60's

The congregation was traditional and did not take to new methods of worship. In the 1960's, some churches were allowing

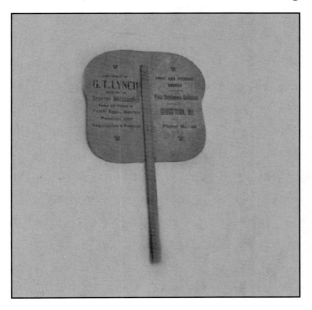

The song book rack on the back of each pew normally had several hand fans. They were usually donated by local businesses which many times were local funeral homes. Photo by the author.

the guitar to be used in the services. That was considered taboo by many of the traditionalists. Several times it was suggested that teen dances be held in our Community Hall. Those suggestions were quickly quashed because dancing was not a proper activity on church property.

Church was much more than just worship on Sundays. The Church was the center of social activity in the neighborhood. We did not go to town for social functions. There were many covered dish dinners in the Community Hall on Friday or Saturday nights. Some areas refer to them as "pot luck dinners." Everyone brought a dish which was then displayed and served buffet style.

Just as special to a young child were the ice cream festivals, where everyone in the neighborhood made homemade ice cream of all flavors and their special recipe cakes and pies. This was a chance in the summer to see friends and play tag and other games.

Obviously, the major religious Christian holidays had special events. The Christmas program consisted of speeches by the Sunday School children, followed by a visit from Santa. Special care was taken to make sure there were extra gifts for children who might be in attendance that night who normally did not attend our Church.

Easter started with a sunrise service, followed by breakfast in the Church Hall. Everyone was there in their Easter clothes.

The Hymnal used by our Church. When new books were purchased current and former parishoners were contacted and asked to "buy" a Hyymnal in memory of, or in honor of, someone and donate it to the Church. Photo by the author.

Bible School started the summer activities. It seemed to start right after school ended, but it was a fun time that was eagerly anticipated. It lasted five days, and the one-half day sessions were filled with crafts, games and Bible stories.

As a very young child, I remember our Church having a softball team. My brother, Merrill, played on the team. The ball field was at Uncle Carlton's and in later years was moved to Steiner's road. Although the team ceased to exist during my pre-teen years, it did revive for a few years in the late 1970s and early 1980s.

Homecoming services were always a special time to reunite with people and relatives one had not seen during the year. Former ministers and Church members came

This is the original Church which was built in 1853 during the pastorate of Reverend John Hough. The three persons pictured are Josiah S. Wilson, John D. Joseph, and Sheppard M. Walls, who served on the building committee to replace this church with the new one that stands today. The current Church is situate to the left of this picture. Compare the location of the tombstone of a cross to the placement of the same tombstone in the picture of the new Church at the beginning of this chapter. Photo from the collection of J. Everett Moore, Sr. and Dorothy M. Moore.

Rural Life in the 1950's and 60's

This is a view from the pulpit on the east end of the Church looking south. There are 3 stained glass windows on each side of the Church. The names of the sponsors of the windows are part of the stained glass. Photo by the author.

to enjoy an afternoon of singing, usually highlighted by outside singers and groups that came to perform. The sermon was usually delivered by a guest minister, often one who had served the Circuit or Charge earlier, followed by a large, covered-dish dinner with everyone's favorite recipes.

There were also Sunday night services. Often these were led by a guest speaker with singing. One special treat was hearing the St. John's Quartet, which sang in the southern Christian quartet style. The members were Rev. Joseph Holiday, Bob West, Ralston Pettyjohn, and Uncle Charles Moore.

As I got older, I became involved with MYF (Methodist Youth Fellowship), which was normally led by the minister and some parents. This was an opportunity to congregate with those of one's own age.

The St. John's Quartet. From left to right; Uncle Charles Moore, Bob West, Ralston Pettyjohn, and Rev. Joe Holliday. Louise Dorey (not pictured) played the piano for the group. They performed not only in our Church but traveled to other Churches in the area. Photo courtesy of Gaye Pettyjohn King.

Growin' Up Country

An early picture of the original St John's Church building. Photo courtesy of Delaware Public Archives.

Rev Joseph N. Geiger served St. Johns from 1964 to 1966. Photo from the collectionl of Mr. and Mrs. J. Everett Moore, Sr.

It was always considered a special day to have the minister and his family over for Sunday dinner after church. Reverend and Mrs. Schultz are guests of Helen Truitt in the Walls Homestead. Rev. Schultz served St. Johns from 1959 to 1962. Photo from the collection of Mr. and Mrs. J. Everett Moore, Sr.

Rural Life in the 1950's and 60's

Rev. Frank Lucia served St Johns from 1956 to 1959. Photo from the collection of Mr. and Mrs. J. Everett Moore, Sr.

Although this picture was taken well before the time frame of this book it does show the long tradition of dinners at the Church. The tables are set for a church social in the grove at St. John's in the 1880s. This is located on the original tract called "Springfield" owned by the Church. Note the horses and buggies hitched to the trees. Also, note that the legs of the tables are made from trunks of small trees. Photo courtesy of Delaware Public Archives.

The Well Sweep

This is a picture of F. Helen Truitt, nee Walls, standing by the well and well sweep in 1962. To the right is the meat or the smoke house, directly behind it was the corn crib, the other buildings were used as stables and as general storage. Photo from the author's collection.

Wall's Homestead

What I now refer to as the "Walls Homestead" had simply been known as "Helen's" when I was growing up. Later in life it became "home" and the place where we raised our children.

Although Helen Truitt, nee Walls and Lilly Stewart were not young or modern, it was an interesting place as a child to visit. Lilly was a companion that lived with Helen for many years. She had been placed in Stockley Center as a young widow with two children and no way to support herself or her children.[1] The Walls family was paid a stipend by the State for keeping her. She actually went to live with Helen's parents, Mr. and Mrs. Sheppard M. Walls, on August 16, 1939. She helped with the chores and many from outside the area thought Helen and Lilly were sisters.

When I moved in, we removed the plaster and the oil space heater and exposed the original fireplace. We found a brick with the date 1813 and a crane for hanging pots. The family indicated that the 1813 date was the date the fireplace was rebuilt. The paneling was painted a faux wood grain maple color. Photo by the author.

---

1. Locally referred to simply as "Stockley" at the time is now known as "The Stockley Center" and at various times known as "The Hospital for the Mentally Retarded". It also served as an alms house for those women who were destitute and unable to care for themselves.

This is the winding stairway in the oldest section of the house. Many years ago, in both 1797 and in 1802 a carpenter kept his time on the underneath of these steps visible in the wood closet. Photo by the author.

In the winter, the home had a special coziness provided by the wood cook-stove in the kitchen and the oil space heater in the living room. Everything was very old. The kitchen had one bureau, a sink with a metal base cabinet, an old corner cupboard that Helen's grandmother had found discarded in a dump, and the wood stove. The floor was linoleum.

The living room had a hand-loomed carpet (as did most of the rooms except the kitchen) over wide-plank, heart-pine floors, many rockers, some straight back wood chairs and most interesting... an oil space heater whose stove pipe was fed into a plastered over fireplace. The wall around the fireplace was wood, Queen Ann style paneling, and the rest of the walls were wallpapered over horse hair plaster.

The upstairs was reached by one of two winding stairways. The stairway, accessible from the living room, was so narrow that one's shoulders touched the wall. The stairway (accessible from the kitchen) was wider but was still a winding stairway. Because of Helen's age and mobility issues, it was extremely rare that she went upstairs.

Although we often visited, most of my memories don't come from "visiting" but from walking over to Helen's to spend some time during the day. I'm sure I was no more than four or five when I started walking to Helen's. Her house was on the adjoining farm, and I walked to the end of our road, currently known as "Deep Branch Road," to the main road ("Springfield Road") and then about one hundred yards or so west to her house.

Helen in front of her chicken house. The left side was open front with roosts and the left side was enclosed and had nests (laying boxes) set up. Photo from author's collection.

Rural Life in the 1950's and 60's

These homemade boxes served as nests for hens to lay their eggs. There were nests such as these set up in all the barns. Photo by the author courtesy of Clark White.

I followed Helen as she did her chores. When older, I helped feed and water her chickens, gather eggs, and helped with her "chicken killings." She had two small chicken houses attached together and a small chicken yard that was fenced in, although she often turned the chickens loose in her yard. She had layer boxes for the hens to lay eggs, not only in the chicken houses, but also in some of the barns. I did help collect eggs and was afraid of some of the hens—they didn't particularly like someone stealing their eggs from under them. I was always on the alert for black snakes that were very fond of the eggs.

As a very young child, I was often fooled by the "china" eggs. They were artificial and placed in the nests to coax the hens to lay eggs.

Helen not only collected eggs for her own use but also sold the eggs to neighbors. If she did not have egg cartons, she put them in Wheaties boxes and wrapped them with string.

I also helped her feed the chickens and put them up to roost for the night and lock the gate. She had "roosts" set up in one of the houses. These were simply poles that had been cut from saplings and tied or nailed for the chickens to roost on at night.

Chickens roosted on poles set in the houses. They actually got up on the poles and slept for the night. Roosts are not used in commercial chicken houses today. Lights are kept on all day so the chickens can eat 24 hours a day. Picture by the author courtesy of Delaware Agricultural Museum and Village.

We often shelled corn for feed. She had a corn sheller that operated by hand crank. An ear of corn was dropped in the top while the crank was being turned, and the shelled individual kernels of corn came out one opening into a bucket that was placed on the ground. The empty corn cob would come out another opening. Even though the crank was hard to turn, it was easier than the alternative which was to shell the ears by twisting them between one's hands.

Helen's big day was her chicken killing day. She got up early and caught a dozen or so hens. She had a unique and efficient system.

a young child as seeing a headless chicken bouncing and running all over the yard.

After the hens were still and all the nerve movement ended, she then started the process of removing the feathers. She poured boiling water into a huge tub. The chickens were then dipped in the water which caused the feathers to slip. We then removed them by the handful. She next ran a flame over the hen's body to singe any remaining pin feathers.

Next, we "cleaned" (gutted) the hens. I don't remember saving the feathers, but nothing usable was thrown away. She ate the feet (many people had chicken feet gravy with their meals) and saved the livers, gizzards and necks.[2] The chickens were then sold to neighbors and some town folks.

Pictured is a corn sheller. The handle was turned and an ear of corn was fed through the top. A bucket was placed under the sheller and the shelled corn dropped into it. The empty cob was discharged through the front opening. Photo by the author courtesy of Irvin and Gaye King.

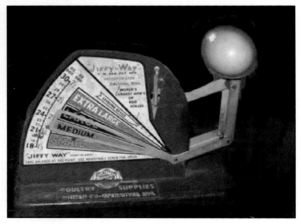

Helen often used a scale, such as this, to grade her eggs. Photo by the author, courtesy of Delaware Agricultural Museum and Village.

Instead of using an ax to cut off the head, as was the tradition in the neighborhood, she had hay-bailing twine nooses to hold the hens upside down by one leg. She had these nooses on her clotheslines and on low hanging limbs on trees. She then donned an oilcloth apron and used a sharp knife as she held the head and cut the head off. Although the head was cut off, it wasn't quite as traumatic for

Years later, when I started title searching in the Court House as part of my clerkship for the Bar, I met Peggy Dunning, who told the story of getting calls from Helen. She often

---

2. Although she and many others ate the necks others used them for for crab bait. In many areas, non-commercial crabbers were referred to as "chicken neckers."

called very early in the morning and stated that she was killing chickens and that they were "good and fat." These were big baking chickens that were used for the regional favorite "chicken and dumplings."

Helen did use a wood cook stove in the kitchen, which meant she had to have wood to burn. Someone always brought her a truck load of wood, which we referred to as slab wood. Slab wood was the strips created with the bark when the saw mill started the board cuts. She often hired someone to split the load of wood, but it was not unusual for me to help split wood and haul it into the house for her use.

Another unique and fun feature at Helen's was the large overhead grape arbor. Although I looked forward to picking grapes when they became ripe in late summer, the real treat was spending a day making grape jelly. Although I don't remember all the particulars, I do know we made it in the "summer kitchen," the room that years later would be my den. I helped pick the grapes, and Mom helped Helen with the preparations. All kinds of glasses and jars were used for the jelly. After they were filled, one of my jobs was to pour hot paraffin wax over the jelly to preserve the jelly. When cooled, it made an airtight seal. This jelly lasted all year.

This is a pitcher top pump. Although it had been replaced in the Walls property they were common in the neighborhood. They had to be primed which meant one had to have a water source to pour down the pump to get it started. One had to be careful in using a pump that was seldom used. Wasps often made nests and they were quick to attack one using the pump. Photo by the author.

The summer kitchen was used in the summer for canning and other cooking chores. It was not insulated and had bare studs and open rafters. It appeared to have been added to connect the original summer kitchen (a separate building) and the milk house to the main house. One wall was clapboard because it was actually the original wall of the house. The original outside window and door were in that original clapboard wall between the modern kitchen and the summer kitchen.

When I was a child, the "modern" kitchen had the wood cook-stove. If used in the summer, the whole house would be unbearably hot. The summer kitchen was thus separate so the cooking would not make the house unbearable in the summer. There was a unique cook-stove in that kitchen, fired by oil or kerosene. It had a separate unit that sat on the burners for an oven.

This is a wringer washer similar to the one Helen owned. Clothes were passed by hand through the rollers at the top to "wring" the water from the clothes before hanging on the line. Photo by the author.

There was also a very large sink built all of wood that took up a large amount of space. Although it was wood, the sink basin was lined with metal. I only remember a faucet in the sink, but my older brothers remember the sink with a pitcher-top hand pump.

She also had a wringer washer there. It was basically a round washing machine on wheels with a wringer on top. When the clothes were finished washing and rinsing, they were manually fed through the wringer which forced the excess water out prior to being hung on the clothes line. I suspect the phrase "been through the wringer" referred to the wringer on a washing machine.

Helen's home was known for the well in the front yard. It had a sweep to retrieve the water. The sweep consisted of a white oak tree trunk with a fork at the top. This was placed in the ground several feet from the well, extending approximately 15 feet into the air. A spruce pine (Virginia Pine) was then placed between the forks extending over the well. A short piece of chain attached a sassafras or cedar pull handle from the pine to the bucket. The long pine was balanced such that a slight pull on the sassafras handle would cause the bucket to descend into the well and a tug would cause the bucket to come back to the top of the well. It was such a well-known landmark that when I told people where I lived, they were aware of the well.

The well itself was constructed of large terra-cotta style tiles that were stacked 2 or 3 deep, resting on green oak boards placed vertically from the bottom of the tiles to the bottom of the pit. When Helen was a child,

Checking the balance and pivot point of the sweep pole to make sure it would, with minimal effort, pull the bucket out of the well filled with water. Photo by Robert Robinson.

Rural Life in the 1950's and 60's

the well was drained by bucket in the summer when the springs were down. Using a ladder, someone would always climb down the well and scrub the oak boards.

Helen only used this well to water her chickens. It was no longer used for household water. Since the advent of electricity, a modern water pump was used to provide household water. In fact, the Walls family was one of the first rural families to have electricity. Prior to the Rural Electrification Act (REA), the Walls family paid to have electricity extended from town to their home.[3]

When I made the farm my home, I replaced the sweep. Jimmie Truitt, Sr, was my advisor on the project, because he had replaced it many times before. There had been articles in the state-wide *Evening Journal*[4] describing the well sweep and its history. It was great to work with "Big" Jimmie on the project. It was he that told me the different types of wood to use on the different parts. He oversaw all aspects of the project.

In the summer, Helen always had a garden. Although it wasn't large, it was bountiful. I helped her till her garden. She had a large, metal-wheel cultivator with several attachments and although it was an antique then, it worked perfectly. It created furrows for planting seed and cultivated between the rows.

The author(on the left) with Jimmie Truitt, Sr. who served as the advisor on the installation of the well sweep. We cut a large white oak tree with a fork for the fulcrum, a spruce (Virginia) pine for the sweep, and a sassafrass or cedar for the hand piece. Jimmie had installed it many times over the years. Photo by Robert Robinson

Three things are memorable, concerning the garden: (1) After working in the garden, we cleaned her tools. She used a piece of brick to clean all the dirt off the metal- be it a hoe, shovel or the cultivator (she also did this to caked on grass on her lawn mower). She then used an oily rag to clean all metal parts. The tools were then stored. (2) Helen covered as much of her skin as possible to keep the sun off. She grew up in a generation when the style for women was to have no tan.

---

3. At the time electricity was provided to some farms by a "Delco". This was a precursor to our modern generators but the electricity was stored in glass batteries. My uncle has often recounted my grandfather getting up from the supper table with the remark "Its time to turn on the Delco." It provided the lights for the home and barn.
4. The News Journal Corporation used to have 2 daily statewide papers....*The Morning News* and *The Evening Journal*. which are described in more detail in the chapter "Newspapers"

To sport a tan would indicate that a female had to work in the fields and thus was of a lesser class. She worked outside with gloves that had the fingers cut out, with sleeves that had been cut from sweaters and a large bonnet. I was usually barefooted in shorts and no shirt. When I asked why she was dressed that way and wasn't she hot, she always responded that she was cooler because the sun did not hit her skin. (3) She was extremely frugal and didn't waste anything. That included available land. Farmers were unable to plant next to telephone poles because their equipment was too large to get close to the poles. Thus, there was an untilled strip next to the poles. Helen had me help her till that strip to plant her pumpkins.

This is the Walls' homestead on February 19, 1907. Pictured from left to right are Sheppard Walls, his brother, Henry, their mother, Mary Jane, seated on the porch, his daughter Helen Walls Truitt, and his wife Ida, nee Conaway. Notice the milk house to the right which is still there, the meat or smoke house on the left, and the 2 hitching posts in front. Later the roof on the right side of the house was raised so that the entire home is now a 2 story home. One can see the slight difference in elevation of the 2 sides today. At that time the inset style porch was done away with and a full front porch was added. The molding in the kitchen still shows evidence of the porch as shown here. Photo from author's collection.

As noted, Helen's frugality extended to other areas. Every feed bag was saved to reuse- in fact, the prior generation used these to make dresses. They had designs and prints and were not made of the burlap that I remember. Some were actually made of linen. The string from the feed bags was also saved. She would save the tops of Wheaties' boxes to wrap the string. As noted before, the Wheaties' boxes (topless) were used to pack

Rural Life in the 1950's and 60's

eggs. When shoes were worn out and could not be resoled anymore, the leather was saved. It made good substitutes for hinges. All tin can lids were cleaned and saved. Many times she would ask me to tack one over holes in her buildings or house. When clothing wore out, the buttons were taken off and saved. The cloth was torn into strips, which were used to crochet into rag rugs. Every jar was saved, cleaned and reused, often for jelly. Old newspapers were used as carpet pads under rugs and also to provide insulation. Nothing was wasted.

Part of the fascination visiting as a child was all the buildings. In addition to the house, there was a milk-house and summer- kitchen attached. There was also the chicken house, three barns, harness shop, shed, corn crib, garage, and a three-seater toilet.[5] There was also an original hitching post with step stone and, of course, the well.

Before I started providing Helen with squirrels, our neighbor Jimmie Truitt, Jr. and my brother Merrill kept her in supply. Every time they took her squirrels, she told them she was going to have a squirrel dinner for them. Merrill told her he didn't like squirrel. Jimmie didn't like squirrel either but had not told her. One day she invited them to dinner and she had squirrel for Jimmie and steak for Merrill. To add insult to injury, she always cooked the squirrel with its head on and used

Some friends visiting Helen on her birthday: from left to right Eunice Smith, Betty Abbott Truitt holding her son, Stephen Truitt, and her daughter, Missy Truitt. The carpet was made by hand on a loom, and the throw rugs were hand made rag rugs. Please note the rockers and straight-back cane bottom chairs. Also note the oil space heater with a stove pipe going into the fireplace. This is the same wall and fireplace shown on page 77. Photo from the author's collection.

a nutcracker to crack open its head so she could pick out and eat the brains. Dad had many years of fun telling Helen every chance he got of how much Jimmie enjoyed the dinner and was looking forward to the next invite.

Not all our visits were fun. More than once Merrill was called to go over to kill a snake that was in the kitchen. On another occasion, I found her pet dog, Brownie, along the side of the road after being hit by a car. I walked her to see him for one last time and then buried her pet and companion. My sister remembers walking over with a two-piece

---

5. Helen did not have an inside bathroom until 1969. In winter and evenings, a commode was used to prevent a cold, dark trip outside. A commode was normally a chair with a chamber pot insert. It was often upholstered to hide the real function.

bathing suit and shirt for a cover up and being promptly scolded for her inappropriate wear which would be tame by today's standards.

I have had the special privilege of living in and making that property my home. Although some changes were made to modernize for today's living, I tried to restore the home to its original beauty.

The Walls family on January 27, 1910. From left to right: Sheppard, Henry, J. Gardner, Mary Jane(their mother) Delphine Pettyjohn, Jeanette Dorman, and Georgia Lank. Photo from the author's collection.

A few years ago I got very serious in searching my family tree. When I searched the ancestry of my paternal grandmother, Ella M. Moore, nee Russell, I found that my children and I are descendants of the Walls family and are direct descendants of the builder of the house. Since construction in the 1700s, the home has always been occupied by direct descendants of the builder.

The original home was probably built by Samuel and Mary Walls, although it is possible that the home was built by Thomas Walls. Samuel (1737-1801) and Mary are buried on the farm at a location I believe to be just northwest of the house.

The family oral history was that a cabin was built and sat at the location of the current structure. The original structure was only the western portion of the current house. The home was at one time a two-story on the west end and a one story on the east end as shown on the photo.

Many of the older farmhouses in the neighborhood had been covered with asbestos shingles, which served as additional insulation. This home was not. It was originally built with cypress shingles on the front and sides which could be seen from the road, and with clapboard in back.

When we started work on the restoration, we tore out the plastered-over fireplace and found a crane still hanging in the fireplace. We were also aware of a brick in one of the closets with the date 1813, which we were told by Helen was the date the fireplace was rebuilt. We also found the "time sheets" of a carpenter on the underside of the winding stairway that noted he had worked there in July of 1802.

Years later, while working in the bedroom of one of my children, I stripped the wall paper and found the signatures of some of

Rural Life in the 1950's and 60's

the prior occupants of the house. They were Eli Walls, James Walls, and Gideon Walls. Although Eli, Sr.[6] (1776 to 1842) could have been one of the signers, it makes more sense that the autographs are those of three of his 11 children, including Eli, Jr.

On another wall, there was a sketch of a person in traditional colonial garb. Rather than covering these up with wallpaper or paint, I had molding placed around them as a frame to preserve this piece of history.

In the summer visitors often socialized on the porch. Few people had air conditioning. Photo from the author's collection.

Sheppard M Walls in front of the house circa 1950. The style was typical of the time; an open front porch, screen dors and windows. The bench is a church pew from the original St. John's Church. Photo from the author's collection.

---

6. Eli Sr was Helen's great grandfather, and Gideon was her grandfather.

WALL'S HOMESTEAD ; PRESENT VIEW

This is the Wall's Homestead as it appears today as my home. The Williamsburg-style raised bed garden to the right is where the chicken houses used to be. The barn to the left was restored by replacing the siding with white oak boards. The small building to the right of the house is the milk house, and the roof line to the left of it is the summer kitchen. Photo from the author's collection.

Rural Life in the 1950's and 60's

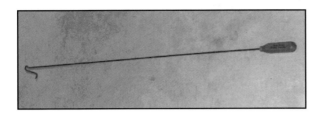

This is a chicken hook. It was a wire with a hook on one end and a handle on the other. One could walk behind a chicken and hook its leg and pull to one. It was often used to catch yard chickens and by servicemen[7] to catch chickens for testing.

This is an egg basket that many used when gathering eggs from their flock. Photo by the author courtesy of Delaware Agricultural Museum and Village.

This is a corn peg used for husking corn. It is a tool that was given to us by the local Indians. Although some are wood, this one has a metal peg and leather strap toin which one inserted one's fingers. Photo by the author courtesy of Jimmie Truitt, Jr.

Sheppard and Ida Walls standing in front of corn shocks in 1943. There were still some farms that harvested the corn in this manner when I was a small boy. The corn was husked, using a corn peg. The ears of corn were then thrown in a pile, and the stalks were cut with a fodder knife and stacked in shocks for feed to the animals at a later time. Photo from the author's collection.

---

7. Service men were the representatives of the poultry integrators. They inspected the farms of the growers on a weekly basis to check the condition of the flock.

Growin' Up Country

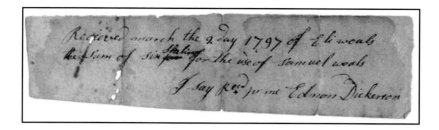

"Received march the 2 day 1797 of Eli walls the sum of six shillings for the use of Samuel Walls   I say read by me Edmon Dickerson". This corresponds with a date written in the Walls homestead as a possible date that the home was built replacing an earlier cabin. All receipts on this page came from the Walls Homestead.

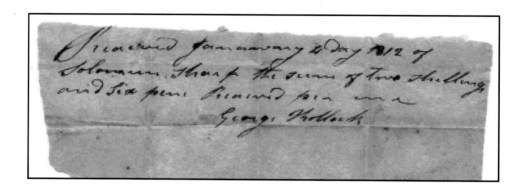

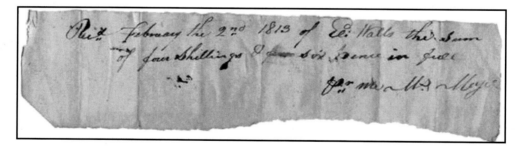

Some receipts were given in todays dollars and cents and others by shillings and pence. Paper was a rare commodity and receipts were often given on small scraps above;. "Paid February the 2nd 1813 of Eli Walls the sum of four shillings and six pence in full". Below:"Received November 23rd,1812 of Soloman Short the sum of twenty nine cents $0.29......."

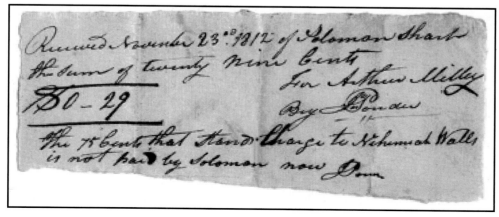

Rural Life in the 1950's and 60's

The Truitt Farm

This is an aerial view of the farm taken in the late 1950's or early 1960's. Directly behind the house was a meat house with a dinner bell beside it. To the right of the meat house was a corn crib, a shed that is largely blocked from view by the tree, and then the dairy barn. The milking took place in this barn and hay was stored in the loft. There are two small chicken houses across Springfield Road in front of the house and one large chicken house behind the house. The fields behind the house were pastures. The large garden was across the road in front of the house and to the left of the chicken houses. The large metal tank at the far left of the chicken house in the foreground is a feed bin. The feed was blown into the tank by large feed trucks, and it was emptied by a gravity chute inside the house by filling a feed cart. Photo courtesy of Jimmie Truitt, Jr.

Jimmie's

The farm I now refer to as the Truitt Farm was simply "Jimmie's" when I was growing up. It was the home of Jimmie and Clara Truitt and their son, Jimmie, Jr., referred to as "the boy" by his father.

The home was a large two-story home surrounded by barns, sheds, chicken houses, corn cribs, pastures, and grain fields.[1] It was directly across the field from our house, and from a very young age, I walked across the field to visit.

Jimmie and Clara Truitt on their 50th wedding anniversary. Photo courtesy of Jimmie Truitt, Jr.

These visits even started preschool.

Although our neighborhood was comprised of farms, Jimmie's was the stereotypical farm. There were chickens, both commercial and yard hens, ducks, guineas,[2] cows, and later sheep. They also had a beautiful collie named, appropriately, Lassie.

Their cattle were part of a diary operation, and they milked the cows twice a day. The cattle often were pastured on the south side

---

1. During the war, two families lived in the house -each with their own kitchen, living room and 2 bedrooms.
2. Guineas are a fowl native to Africa. They have dark meat and many enjoy them with dumplings. They eat bees and ticks and can not be placed near bee hives for that reason

of Springfield Road (the house and milking sheds were on the north side) and the traffic had to be stopped twice a day as the cattle crossed the road. In fact, there was a cattle-crossing sign on Springfield Road. There was little traffic and at times I helped stop the cars.

My first recollection is of milking stalls in one side of a barn. At that time, all milking was done by hand while seated on a small stool. When the cows were ready to be milked, a chain device was placed on the rear legs to keep them from kicking. The cows were milked twice a day—early in the morning and in the late afternoon. When that barn was destroyed, they built a milking parlor that allowed them to use automatic milkers and to milk two cows at a time. The milk was placed next to the road in metal milk cans for the large dairy operation to pick up. The dairy business is very labor intensive and ended when Jimmie, Sr had a heart attack. Jimmie, Jr. was in college at the time. They then started raising sheep, both for the wool and for the meat. They had approximately 50 sheep, and they too were sometimes pastured across the road.

After milking the milk was placed in cans such as this to be picked up by the dairy for processing. Theirs was a small operation by today's standards and they produced approximately two cans per day. Photo by the author.

Signs like these faced east and west on Springfield Road at the Truitt farm. Cattle crossed the road in back the morning and evening for milking.

All the animals, tractors, equipment and buildings made it a fascinating and fun place for a young boy. I followed Jimmie, Sr., Clara and Jimmie, Jr[3] around the farm as they performed their chores. Often, Jimmie, Sr. allowed me to get on the tractor with him. He was the most easy going, laid back (before the term laid back was in vogue) person I have

The tools of the milking trade. The kickers to the left, a milking stool, and a good strong grip were needed for milking cows. The kickers were placed on the rear legs of a cow before she was milked to prevent her from kicking. The stool is very short, approximately a foot high, to put the milker at the appropriate height for milking. Photo by the author courtesy of Jimmie Truitt Sr.

---

3. In the tradition of the neighborhood they were referred to as big Jimmie and little Jimmie, even though little Jimmie was bigger than big Jimmie.

Rural Life in the 1950's and 60's

ever known. I never saw him mad...in fact, his family only remembered seeing him mad twice. One of those occasions was when his dog bit his future son-in-law, Harold King. He was kind, soft spoken and quick to smile.

In addition to her household duties, Clara also worked on the chores. Her home was absolutely spotless and her meals delicious. They had a large garden, and in the summer, they ate fresh vegetables from that garden. In the winter, they ate what she canned and stored in the freezer. She canned string beans, lima beans and corn, and made relish, just to name a few. She also put up pickled watermelon rind. Like her husband, she was quick to smile followed by an infectious laugh.

Clara was from a large family and two of her siblings no longer lived in the area. A brother lived in the Newport News, Virginia area and a sister lived in Philadelphia, Pennsylvania. Both siblings, like their sister, Clara, were jovial and always had a smile.

Her sister, Catherine (nicknamed Cack) and her husband, Al, spent their two-week vacations with Jimmie and Clara. They pitched in and worked on the farm and kitchen, on whatever projects were underway. Jimmie, Jr. remembers that they never seemed like guests or company; they were like other members of the household.

Al worked as a machinist, and one summer he built a corn and a hay-bale elevator for use on the farm. Cack had her sister's infectious laugh, and it was fun as a young child to see them each summer.

Both Jimmie Sr. and Jr. loved to hunt and were very proficient hunters. Jimmie often hosted hunters from town, especially for bobwhite quail. Although he was older than many who joined him on the hunt, the word was that he walked and hunted all his companions into the ground.

Deer hunting was a new activity at that

Jimmie's International 300 tractor pulling a New Idea corn picker. Jimmie used this tractor for plowing, planting, cultivating, and general utility work around the farm. Photo by the author.

time, but both father and son were soon recognized in the neighborhood as the best. Soon, many, including me, wanted to hunt with them to learn their secrets of success. In fact, it is from them that I obtained my love of the outdoors and hunting.

Their prowess in the woods provided a bountiful supply of rabbit, squirrel, quail, and deer. Those along with the chicken, duck, guinea, and beef they raised, provided the meat to go along with their garden bounty for their meals.

This is a pull-behind combine similar to the one that Jimmie's had when I was a young boy. Later, they obtained a self-propelled combine. Photo by the author.

Jimmie's Case 400 tricycle-front tractor was used for plowing and disking. It blew up while Jimmie, Jr. was plowing the back field. Photo by the author.

Rural Life in the 1950's and 60's

Georgetown School

This view of the school was taken from West Market Street nears its intersection with School Lane. This building housed all 12 grades and is the school that the author and his siblings attended for their elementary, junior high and high school years. Photo from the author's collection.

School

My children all attended pre-school and kindergarten before actually starting school. Neither my brothers, sister nor I attended either preschool or kindergarten. We had neither a middle school nor separate elementary and high schools. All of us attended grades one through twelve in the large, brick building on Georgetown's West Market Street that now houses Georgetown Elementary and Middle Schools. When entering the Pine Street entrance, the hallway to the right housed the grades seven through twelve and the hallway to the left was for grades one through six.

I graduated from Georgetown High School (GHS) whose mascot was the Golden Knight. That was before school consolidation combined many of the old, separate school districts into larger entities. Other local schools at that time were Milton, Lewes, and Rehoboth, which later joined to form Cape Henlopen; Bridgeville and Greenwood, which later joined to form Woodbridge; and Millsboro, Lord Baltimore, Selbyville, and John M. Clayton, which later combined with Georgetown to create the Indian River School District.

As noted previously, we lived on Road 315 just off Road 47. The bus picked us up on Road 47. We knew that once the bus stopped to pick up Bobby and Betty Perry, we needed to leave

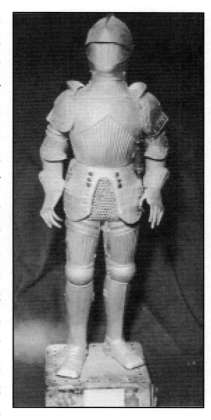

The school mascot, The Golden Knight, stood in the Pine Street lobby separating the Jr. High and Sr. High from the Elementary school. Photo from the Golden Herald.

the house to walk down the road to meet the bus. Our bus ride was only approximately 20 minutes.

In those days, there was a big difference between being from town or from the country when it came to school. We all attended the same building, so there was no need for separate buses for elementary and high school. The day was considered too long for the First and Second Graders, so we were excused at 2:30, when all other grades had to stay until 3:30. Since we all rode the same buses as the older children, we had a dilemma. Therefore, town kids either walked home or their parents picked them up at 2:30 pm. The country kids—and that is how we were known—stayed until 3:30, but had a recess for that last hour.

In elementary school, we had two twenty minute recess periods per day, except for First and Second Grades, when country kids had the extra third recess at the end of the day. I was shocked to learn, when my children started school, that often they would not have a single recess because of the amount of work they had to complete.

Our playground equipment would not pass the consumer safety standards of today. The entire area under the equipment was paved, including under the swings, slide and monkey bars. There was nothing soft to fall on when one fell. We also had a large adjacent field, on which we played tag, football, or kickball (no one knew anything about soccer), or just talked to friends.

We often heard stories of Mom's experiences traveling to school. Her first school until Eighth Grade was near Fairmount on the northeast corner of the intersection of Holly Mount and Beaver Dam Roads. Then she went to Millsboro School. She was raised by a family on Avalon Road and had to walk through the woods to Route 30 between St. John's and Zoar Churches near Kawan Acres Development. She reminded us how lucky we were to be able to see the bus coming, and to have only a short walk to meet the bus.

Each school day started with the Lord's Prayer and salute to the Flag. Our grades in the First and Second Grades were S for satisfactory and U for unsatisfactory. From the 3rd grade on, the grades were the traditional A, B, C, or D. My teachers for my elementary years were First,

This is the first school to bear the name Georgetown School. It was built in 1885 near St. Paul's Episcopal Church on Pine Street. Prior to that, the education of the youth took place in private homes and churches. In 1836, The Old Academy on Race and Pine Streets was constructed(which incidently later was owned and served as a law office for the author). The building that replaced the Old Academy is now used as the Masonic Lodge in Georgetown until the building above was contstructed. Photo from author's collection.

Rural Life in the 1950's and 60's

This building served as the Fairmount School for my mother until the 8th grade. It is located at the northeast corner of Beaver Dam and Holly Mount Roads, east of Indian Mission Church. It now serves as Mount Holly Church. Photo by the author.

purchase $25.00 U. S. Savings Bonds. We bought stamps for either 10 or 25 cents each and placed them in our book. When they were full, we redeemed them for a $25.00 Saving Bond.

Current events were an important part of our curriculum. In the younger grades, we had the "Weekly Reader" and "Highlights for Kids."[1] In the later years of elementary and junior. high, we regularly watched newsreels, called "The 20th Century," to keep us up on current events.

Betty Veasey; Second, Myrtle Jefferson; Third, Ruth Lingo; Fourth, Helen Cober; Fifth, Madeline Richardson; and Sixth, Mary Keeler.

We took the traditional reading, writing and arithmetic with spelling and Delaware history added in. In arithmatic we were required to learn the "times" tables for multiplication.

In the First and Second Grade, we printed. In the Third Grade, we learned to "write" (cursive), which is becoming a lost art. Recently, I conducted a real estate closing in my office, and a graduate student had difficulty writing because she communicates entirely by text or email.

We were taught saving at an early age. In the 3rd grade we bought stamps to purchase U.S. Savings Bonds. The stamps came in 25 cent and 10 cent denominations. When the book was full it was exchanged for a $25.00 Savings Bond. From the author's collection.

The Third Grade was also the grade that taught us the importance of saving. We were given Stamp Books that were used to

One sign of the times was the air raid drills which required us to get under our desk and to protect our heads. This was during the cold war and a time in which World War II was still a recent memory for our parents.

---

1. The father of Rick Bell of Lewes, our former Recorder of Deeds and owner of Harvard Business Services, Inc., was President of Highlights for Kids, Inc. for 25 years and the Chairman of the Board for another 25 years. He served from 1954 until his death in 2010.

Growin' Up Country

The Cuban missle crisis occured when I was in the Seventh Grade. I remember Dad moving the radio into the utility room and leaning on the washer as he and Mom intently listened to President Kennedy's speech. It was a somber atmosphere and both were clearly worried. Even though I was only in the Fifth Grade, it was the topic on everyone's lips the next day. It was not uncommon to hear of talk about bomb shelters, and there were civil defense talks at the PTA to discuss home bomb shelters and how to prepare home emergency kits in case of attack.

There were no computers and all keyboarding was performed on typewriters similar to the one above. Many academic students took personal typing to assist them in college while the secretarial classes took typing I and II.

We had lunches in the cafeteria, and the teachers ate there as well. For 25 cents one could get a platter which included a meat, starch, vegetable, desert and a bottle of milk. Other options were to buy sandwiches or bring one's own lunch. There were no vending machines to tempt students. We were often reminded that we got great meals at a reasonable price because of the federal surplus food program.

In Junior High and High School, there was a period after lunch when we had a break in the Health Room. Many of the girls danced while many of the boys climbed the peg board or just stood around and talked to friends.

There was an entirely different outlook in school. The schools were small (my Class of 1968 was the first to hit 100) and there was not as much concern for safety or discipline as there is now. If there was a problem, the faculty took care of it immediately and forcefully if necessary. I knew everyone in my class and knew by sight everyone in grades Seven through 12. After all, we saw each other every day.

Another difference was that students who flunked actually were held back a grade and had to repeat it.

There were no shorts, tee shirts, shirts with slogans, or plunging necklines. Such dress was considered disruptive and disrespectful and would result in either being sent home to change, a detention, or, at worst, a suspension.

There was little tolerance of those who did not follow the social norms of the day. Girls who became pregnant were suspended from school. It was apparently felt that they were bad examples.

The social norms of the time also dictated that there were traditional roles for men and women. The girls took Home Economics and Shorthand classes in high

Rural Life in the 1950's and 60's

Some of the female members of the Class of '68. Please note the required gym uniforms for girls. Photo from the Golden Herald.

school and the boys took Shop. The girls even had special uniforms they were required to wear in gym class.

Another example of a different societal viewpoint was that on more than one occasion, the boys were invited to bring screwdrivers to school. One time it was to assemble the bleachers in the new field house and another to assemble seats in the grandstand at the Georgetown Raceway. In that case, the boys were allowed to leave school early and get paid to help. In today's climate, anyone that brought a screwdriver would be expelled and arrested for bringing a dangerous weapon to school.

There were no computers nor calculators. The typewriters we used in typing classwere manual and adding machines were used by the staff. We learned to use slide rules in some of the higher math and science classes. Handouts were not photocopied but printed on mimeograph machines and there were no fax machines. Research papers meant reaching for the World Book or Encyclopedia Brittannica.

In high school, there were three main areas of study: Academic, for those planning to go to college, Secretarial, and Vocational. Those classmates in the Vocational program were bussed to the vocational school, now known as Sussex Tech, which served all the schools in the county. They took the core course in our school, and then learned a trade at the vocational school. The courses offered were Auto Body and Fender, Auto Mechanics, Beauty Culture, Commercial Foods, Distributive Education, Drafting, Farm Mechanics, Machine Shop, Mill and Cabinet, Practical Nursing, Electronics, Welding, Barbering, Building Construction, and Industrial Electricity.

Above are 2 shop projects of the author's. The top is a teapot pot holder which taught basic coping saw skills. The bottom is a cutting board made from 3 pieces of wood and a slit mouth insert and plug for the eye. It taught skills such as dowelling pieces together, using a band saw, plug cutter, drill press and a rasp. Photo by the author

Growin' Up Country

We had the standard sports, baseball for the boys and softball for the girls, track for the boys, girl's and boy's basketball, football and wrestling for the boys. Girls particpated in field hockey and cheerleading. One of the high points for any athlete was to earn a "Letter." It was normally given based on the number of quarters or innings played and also given to all seniors. Many bought letter sweaters or had them sewn to their school jacket. In addition to the icon for the sport in which the letter was earned, there was a bar given for each year the person earned a letter.

There were both varsity and junior varsity (referred to as J.V.) squads for all of the above—except track which was new. I had Physical Education (Phys. Ed., P.E. or Gym) all 12 years of school. At least nine of those 12 years, the teacher was Herman Bastianelli, a true legend in downstate coaching. In Eigth and Ninth Grade, he was my football coach. He had a five-year winning streak in J.V. football. He also brought the sport of wrestling downstate and was the coach of both the J.V. and Varsity wrestling teams. They both had five-year win streaks as well . This win streak occured at the same time that he had the win streak in J. V. football.

Herman Bastianelli was an institution at Georgetown School. He taught Physical Education to all 12 grades from 1953 to 1969 and from 1969 to 1984 taught grades 10-12 at Sussex Central High School. He also taught health classes and was very emphatic in his anti tobacco message. He started the wrestling team in 1960 and starting the 2nd year had an undefeated team for 6 straight years, 56 straight wins and 8 conference championships. He had a total record of 150 wins and 15 losses in his 16 year career as wrestling coach. He also coached J.V. wrestling at the same time and had equally impressive records. He also had 5 undefeated J.V. football teams, several undefeated baseball teams and a state championship cross country team. He was inducted into both the State Wrestling Hall of Fame and the Delaware Sports Hall of Fame. He maintained a vigorous exercise routine, even working out on the universal weights with his teams. He also rode a single speed bike 5 miles to school everyday. When he turned 70, his wife took him to Ocean City, Maryland. He warmed up, did 100 pushups in the sand and then swam to the Delaware Seashore Park. He and the love of his life, Marie, are often seen on local dance floors. It is both a source of enjoyment and a way to keep fit. He is a man respected and admired by all. Photo courtesy of Herman Bastianelli.

Rural Life in the 1950's and 60's

Fall in a small town meant the start of football season. It seemed the entire community turned out for the games, and the local and statewide papers provided coverage. The 7th to 12th graders participated in pep rallys every Friday afternoon in the auditorium. The coach and team captain normally commented on the upcoming game, and the cheerleaders led cheers. Everyone left the auditorium excited for game time to start.

Although basketball was the traditional winter sport, Mr. Bastianelli created a wrestling dynasty that rivaled football's excitement. He had pep rallys and special events. Wrestlers wore their warmup shirts to school the day of meets, and most importantly, he achieved success. In addition to his win streak, he had a host of current and former state champion wrestlers that helped build excitement and expectations.

I wrestled in the 10th grade through my senior year. In my senior year, I dropped a weight class and actually wrestled in the 112 lb weight class. In the beginning of the season, I was allowed to weigh up to 114 lbs; and after approx 1/2 the season, we were allowed an extra pound, and I could weigh up to 115 lbs and still make weight. We were weighed in shortly before the meet with both coaches looking on. There were many days that I stepped on the scales with an orange to see if I could make weight if I ate it.

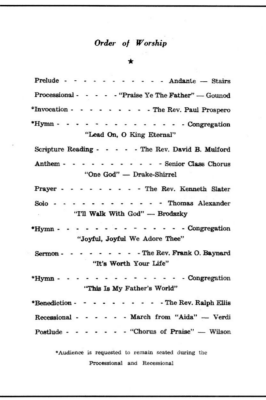

This is the program from our Baccularuate Service in the spring of 1968. It is apparent that religious topics were permitted. From the author's collection.

Some other activites in addition to sports were Band, Chorus, Future Teachers of America, Future Farmers of America, Student Council, Athletic Council, Band Council, Candy Stripers, American Field Service (which sponsored the Foreign Exchange Student), Library Club, Service Club, French Club, The Golden Herald Staff (Yearbook), Stage Crew, Plays and the National Honor Society.

When my oldest brother graduated, there was a "Rifle Club" and students actually had target practice.

Our senior year was a big deal and filled with anticipation. There was an excitement in the air as we finally arrived at the top of the pecking order. We had many experiences

This is the Pine Street entrance to the school. The hallways to the right led to the Jr. and Sr. High classes and the hallway to the left led to the Elementary classes and the cafeteria. Photo courtesy of Delaware Public Archives.

that were for seniors only. One was meeting a new classmate, the foreign exchange student. During our senior year, our exchange student was Nuth Napan, from Thailand, who lived with the Raymond Rust Family.[2] We received our class rings on Ring Day, which included a formal ceremony and a speaker. We also had senior pictures. Prayer was not an issue but a given, so we did have a baccalaurette service. Graduation was a solemn ceremony without the cheering that one hears at today's events.

Upon completion of high school, my classmates went to college (many went to DTCC, which was starting its second year), the military (Vietnam was raging), entered the workforce, and/or got married. The biggest employer at that time was the DuPont Company's nylon plant in Seaford, Delaware.

We went into the world with a very positive and patriotic message...respect authority, the U.S. was the greatest country in the history of the world, and anyone could do anything they wanted as long as they kept their nose clean and worked hard.

---

2. His American "brother" was Tommy Rust, a junior. The AFS always placed the exchange student in a home with a student of the same sex in the junior year to prevent head to head competion with two seniors in the same household. They knew the senior year was important and felt the american student should not have to share that experience with the exchange student. In my junior year our family was host to Jose Gibson from Lima, Peru.

Rural Life in the 1950's and 60's

Fire Prevention Week was much anticipated by the elementary kids. We got to visit the fire house and take a ride on a fire truck. We also wrote essays and the winner from each grade was recognized at a ceremony in school with the Fire Company leaders. Please note that kids were even allowed to ride atop the cab of the fire truck. Those in the photo below are back row, l-r.Alvin Mumford, Reverend Mulligan, Herb Von Goeres, and Bob Vanaman; kneeling row l-r; William Sturgis, Gaye Pettyjohn King, Marion Shockley, Pat Pennell, Barbara Hazzard, Elaine Eckstorm, and Judy Layton. Photos courtesy of Delaware Public Archives.

The Store

The store as it appeared in the 1950's and 60's. There was a gas pump in front until the early 1990's. Note the kerosene pump to the left in front of the store which still remains. This is the third location for this building which started as Springfield School 33.

Wilson's Store

Most neighborhoods had their local country store. There was Stell Rogers' Store at Mount Joy, Tom Best's Store in Nassau, and Oliver Jones' Store and Workman's Store west of Georgetown, to name a few. We had Wilson's Store at Springfield Crossroads.

Wilson's store began as a one room school known as Springfield District #33. During its time as a school, it was located approximately a quarter of a mile west of its current location on the north side of Springfield Road, according to the 1868 Beers Atlas.

Sometime between 1930 and 1933, it was purchased by F. Helen Truitt, nee Walls, and her husband, Francis Truitt. They moved the building approximately one mile west of its current location to a spot on the south side of Springfield Road. It was located at the approximate location of Wayne Rust's stock car garage today. At that time, it was known as Truitt's Store.

In 1941, the store building made its final move to its current location by new owner Everett Johnson. The date is still evident in the concrete front step to the store. Everett Johnson also operated a garage on the site. The concrete pad to the north of the store building marks the site of the garage. He also had my uncle, Carlton Moore, cutting hair on the corner to help bring business to the location. Dad helped move a small brooder house to the store corner, and they fixed it up with a small stove and barber's chair. Uncle Carlton was in school at the time and also played both football and baseball. He still cut hair three nights a week and Saturdays. Because of his schedule, people would often be waiting an hour or so for him to get there. They would wait in the store, thus increasing its business.

Marshall Wilson bought the store in December, 1944. Marshall had a large family, and his goal was simply to earn enough from the store to cover food costs and spending money for his family.

Wilson's was not the busy place it is now.[1] There was no grill or subs nor was it referred to as Wilson's or Wilson's Store ...it was simply "The Store." It was a place to congregate and talk to neighbors and to pick up a soft drink and snack. There were gas pumps out front. There was an old stuffed chair, in which by tradition the oldest person was allowed to sit. I remember Jim West, Paynter (Paint) Joseph, Basil Perry, and my grandfather, Carroll Wilson, at times sitting there. It was fun as a child hearing what the old-timers had to say about the affairs of the world. Our universe was small, and most discussions centered around the crops, weather or local gossip.

In the summer, we discussed whose corn would tassel first, who would have the first sugar corn[2], or who would grow the biggest tomatoes. If it was dry, the drought was compared to other memorable droughts. If there was rain, it seemed that all wanted the bragging rights to have received the most rain.

In the winter, the discussions were about the coldest winters or the winter with the most snow. These tales seemed embellished even to a young child. It seemed that everyone walked miles to school through neck-deep snow.

Marshall Wilson sold cigars by the box or individually with by far most being sold individually. All the local kids asked for the empty cigar boxes to hold treasures such as baseball cards, arrowheads, and the like. Our parents often used them to store bolts, screws and small parts. Photo by the author.

It was a place where one could redeem soft drink [3] bottles for money, buy 22 caliber bullets by the individual bullet and where those who smoked could buy one individual cigarette.

At that time, regular soft drinks were only six cents, and the eight ounce Cokes were five cents if you drank them in the store. If you took the bottle with you, the deposits were three cents and two cents, respectively. In fact, many of us would ride our bikes for hours, looking for discarded soft drink bottles along the roadside. We often found enough to buy a drink and some penny candy and have extra change for spending money.

---

1. To give an example of how quiet it was compared to the busy store of today, I remember when Richard Wilson, Jim's older brother, took over the store after he got back from the Army. The store activity was slow enough that he also "Simonized" cars in the summer under the tree in the parking lot to earn additional money.
2. Sugar corn was the term used for what we now refer to as sweet corn.
3. We always used the term "soft drink", not "soda" or "pop"

Rural Life in the 1950's and 60's

The store was open from 6:00 am to 7:30 pm five days per week and on Saturdays from 6:00 am to 6:00 pm. On many holidays, including the Fourth of July and Thanksgiving, the store was open until 10:00 am.

The Wilson children worked at the store during the summers. The oldest—the "boss"—received seven dollars and fifty cents per week. The next in age received two dollars and fifty cents per week for a five-day week. When the oldest obtained employment elsewhere, the helper would be promoted to "boss" and the next in line became the helper.

Jim Wilson, the current owner, bought the store from his father in 1970. He started making subs in 1971 and added a grill in 1974. As a result, his business really soared. He is well known for the size of his breakfast sandwiches and subs.

When Jim married, he and his wife, Lynette, put a mobile home to the north of the store on the concrete pad that was once Everett Johnson's garage. They later built a home across Springfield Road where they reside to this day.

Jim Wilson guarding his cash register while sporting his ever present revolver on his hip. The shelves are original from when it was first opened as a store in the 1930s. The display case behind Jim was filled with candy when I was a child. Photo by the author

Jim is one that still practices the same frugality that everyone did when I was young. When the weather is bad, Jim puts old newspapers on the floor instead of rugs. He still cuts up used cigarette cartons and uses the backs to write notes and make signs for the store. He recycles his rubber bands and writes his sandwich orders on strips of paper instead of wasting whole sheets of paper.

The Store is thriving and is the only place I know where you can get your meal, have documents notarized and buy a gun.

SPRINGFIELD FREE SCHOOL #33

This photo was taken the last day of school in Springfield Free School #33. All the neighborhood were in attendance, including many of the author's ancestors. Photo courtesy Gay Pettyjohn King.

BRANCHES TAUGHT

Reading
Writing
Spelling
Written Arithmetic
Mental Arithmetic
Grammar
Geography
U.S. History.

Above left is the shool after it closed but before it took on new life as "Truitt's Store". Photo courtesy of Delaware Public Archives. Above right is part of the quarterly report shown on the next page. The teacher listed the subjects taught that quarter. From the author's collection.

Rural Life in the 1950's and 60's

Quarterly Report of Springfield School. District No. 33, in Sussex County, for the Quarter ending February 18, 1881.

This is the heading of the Quarterly Report for Springfield School #33, for the quarter ended February 1881. Other report cards in the my collection refer to the school as St John's School #33 even though the correct name was Springfield School.

> The winter has been very severe, and hence the want of proper attendance; my scholars being mostly small

The teacher noted why her students had a poor attendance for the quarter. It reads: "The winter has been very severe, and hence the want of proper attendance; my scholars being mostlly small."

No.	Names of Males.	First Month Atten'ce	Second Month Atten'ce	Third Month Atten'ce	Average per Quarter	No.	Names of Females.	First Month Atten'ce	Second Month Atten'ce	Third Month Atten'ce	Average per Quarter
1	Truitt Pettyjohn	7	18	16	41	1	Ida P. Atkins	14	10	16	40
2	David Pettyjohn	8	17½	16½	42	2	Emma Rogers	10	4	15	29
3	John W. Rogers	10	5	15	30	3	Henrietta Cooper	16	14	18	48
4	Soudie West	13½	10	16½	40	4	Sissa Jefferson		5	16	22
5	Marquis E. Rogers	8	5	15	28	5	Sarah Derrickson		4	5½	13½
6	Charlie T. Atkins	18	14	20	52	6	Jenette Walls	7	4	14	25
7	Harry W. Smith		14	19	33	7	Ellie Atkins	6		1	7
8	Alexander Walker		7	13	20						
9	Wilber Cooper		6½	15	21½						
10	Louis V. Derrickson		4	12	16						

Records from Springfield School #33. Wilber Cooper, my great grandfather, is the ninth name on the list above. Photo from the author's collection.

The Moore Household At Christmas

From left: Merrill, me in my Davy Crocket suit and with an accordian, Teresa and Ronald. Note the rounded TV screen and the lack of wall to wall toys one would see today. Photo from the author's collection.

Holidays

Our school holidays were Thanksgiving, Christmas vacation, Easter vacation (starting on Good Friday), George Washington's birthday (celebrated on February 22), and Lincoln's birthday (celebrated on February 12) There was no winter break, spring break, and Presidents Day. Ours was a time before political correctness.

We did go trick-or-treating, but as country kids, it was very limited. We only visited relatives and people we knew in the neighborhood. Our main Halloween event was a party in the Church Community Hall where many adults also dressed in costumes and participated in games, including bobbing for apples.

Teresa and me on Christmas morning. Photo from the author's collection.

Christmas was the most anticipated holiday starting in the fall with the delivery of the Sears and Montgomery Wards catalogs commonly referred to as "Wish Books."

Our Christmases were pale in comparison (in regards to the amount of gifts) to those of today. My children and now my grandchildren get more gifts on a birthday than we did for Christmas. It was tradition in our household to get one "big" gift, normally a toy, and the rest of the gifts were clothes or things with a practical purpose.

During this time of year, we were reminded to be thankful for what we had. We heard stories of how my mother was so poor that one year all she got was a sweet potato in her stocking. She also told of her best Christmas ever when she got one gift—a baby carriage which she used to cart her kittens around the yard. Most of all, we were told to be thankful for our family because our mother, an only child, lost her mother when she was just seven years old.

Every child was excited when Santa's house appeared in the circle. Santa would meet and greet local children at this loation. Photo courtesy of the Delaware Public Archives.

We did decorate the house, but our efforts were not extravagant. We placed candles in the kitchen windows and in later years in the living room windows. We did not decorate the outside of the house with lights or other decorations......it was thought to be a waste of electricity.

We would often hang a wreath on our door that was freshly made either with holly, crows foot or turkey beard. Our area was well known for its wreath-making and many of the older residents still plied the craft. My grandfather, Carroll Wilson, often made the holly wreaths, and he would tell of people making large quantities (especially in the Route 5 area between Hollymount and Milton) and shipping them to the city for sale.

We did not buy a precut tree nor did we cut our tree at a tree farm. We searched the woods and cut our own tree. Dad and Uncle Charles owned a farm we referred to as the "Hyland Smith" farm that had naturally growing white pines. Many others in the area cut red cedar for their Christmas trees. Not only did we cut our own tree, but we also often cut a tree for my classroom at school. Every classroom had its own tree, and the trees were usually brought in by a parent of one of the students.

Christmas day, after the opening of the gifts, was spent receiving visitors—uncles, aunts, and cousins—and then later visiting them.

Although Christmas and Easter were both religious holidays, I remember Easter more as a Church event. We did receive the traditional Easter candy in the Easter baskets, but even then it was not nearly as commercialized as Christmas. Many people actually received live "chicks" for Easter that were dyed different colors. They were purchased at Grant's or Woolworth stores. Sunday Church service was special, and everyone wore their spring finest. There was normally a sunrise service followed by breakfast in the Church Hall. It seemed the entire neighborhood was there.

Rural Life in the 1950's and 60's

Many in the area went to Rehoboth Beach on Easter to participate in the Easter Parade and Promenade on the boardwalk. The winners of the different categories, e.g., boy, girl, man, woman, usually had their picture in the paper, wearing their Easter finest. That is not an event in which we participated.

On July 4th we always went to Trap Pond for a picnic and swim. The park had playground equipment, ball fields, picnic tables and grills, limited camping (tent), and a lifeguard. At that time, the area was segregated with the "colored" area located on the opposite side of the pond. Photo postcard from the author's collection.

I do not remember either Memorial Day or Labor Day as being different from any other day, except to signal the start and end of the summer visitors to our beach as well as a start and end of the school year.

The most anticipated day of the summer, other than my birthday, was the Fourth of July. We always went to Trap Pond State Park for a picnic and swim. We usually left home around 10:00 or 11:00 am. Dad always had work or chores to take care of before we left, and mom fried chicken and did the preparation of the picnic basket, which seemed to take forever.

Although I certainly anticipated Christmas the most, and Easter was a welcome sign of spring after the long winter months, and Fourth of July was a fun summer break, I would have to classify Thanksgiving as my favorite holiday. It was a day of cooking and preparation. We hosted the dinner; thus, our home was the hub of Thanksgiving

A young girl and mother showing off her trophy for being the best dressed young girl. There were trophies given for many categories including best dressed couple, best dressed family, etc. Photo courtesy of Rehoboth Beach Historical Society.

preparations and activity. We put the leaves in the table and set up additional tables for all the guests. When my cousins arrived, we played football until called for dinner. The atmosphere was filled with excitement, stimulated by the aromas for the long awaited dinner. Dinner always consisted of turkey, dumplings, dressing, potatoes, sweet potatoes, applesauce and cranberry sauce (the only time of the year we had it), and Aunt Hilda always baked her tasty merengue pies. Because of the number of people, we filled two rooms—the kids in one room and the adults in the other. After dinner, the adults sat around, talked and had coffee. The kids played games, and, if we were lucky, Pop Pop Larry Moore played a game of checkers with us.

The recollections of the day are painted in my mind like a Norman Rockwell picture.

The nativity scene was annually featured on the circle with large life size figures. Photo courtesy of the Delaware Public Archives.

People from throughout the state flocked to Rehoboth Beach on Easter morning to participate in the annual Easter Promenade. Prizes were given to the best couple, best dressed children, and also for unique hats and bonnets. Photo courtesy of Delaware Public Archives.

Rural Life in the 1950's and 60's

Gardens

This is a traditional row-style garden. Onions are in the foreground followed by newly set strawberries, cabbage, and tomatoes in the next row. The poles are for lima beans (often called pole or butter beans). Strings were tied between poles for the beans to climb. An established strawberry bed is located after the first row of pole beans followed by corn in the back. Photo by the author courtesy of Jimmie Truitt, Jr.

Gardens

Most people in the neighborhood had gardens, and the ones that did not were sure to receive plenty of fresh vegetables from those who did. Everyone shared their surplus. In the spring, it would not be uncommon to see Mr. Marvel (Rodney Jr.'s grandfather) traveling the roads with his Farmall Cub tractor, going from farm to farm to plow gardens for people. Others simply used a shovel to turn the earth.

Everyone wanted to get the jump on spring and to plant the garden as soon as possible. Even though gardens entailed a lot of hard work, people enjoyed the work in their gardens. Work in the garden signaled an end to winter and start of the coming spring. However, gardening was not a hobby. Gardens were an important source of food for the entire year.

Peas are very cold-tolerant and were usually the first crop planted, followed by onions and then cabbage. Certain plants such as tomatoes, peppers and cabbage, were transplanted directly into the garden instead of planted as seed. Though these plants could be started at home indoors or in a cold frame, I believe most in the neighborhood bought them from a local Southern States store or a local greenhouse. Often, early tomato plants were covered with a basket (often referred to as a peach or 5/8 basket) secured with a brick on top. This protected the plant at nights from the colder temperature and protected them from wind-blown dirt during the day. The basket was removed for a longer and longer time each day until it was no longer needed.

We did not plant by the moon but many did.[1] Root crops were planted when the moon was on the decrease, and plants that grew above the ground were planted when the moon was on the increase.

---

1. Some even used the moon to determine when to dig a hole. They would dig when the moon was on the increase, otherwise they said, there would not be enough dirt to fill it back in.

Growin' Up Country

Most gardeners had access to stable manure to fertilize the garden, although commercial fertilizer and lime were also used. That was used instead of chicken manure on the gardens. The straw mix with the stable manure was deemed better than the sawdust mix with the chicken manure. The chicken manure was normally used on the fields. Although I am sure that some may have had a mulch pile, I was not aware of anyone having such a pile and believe I was in college before I heard the term.

Certain crops such as squash, cucumbers, watermelons, and cantaloupes, were planted in hills, while others were planted in rows, e.g., corn, string beans, bush lima beans, radishes and carrots. Pole limas (often referred to as butter beans) were actually planted in hills next to poles set in rows. People cut saplings in the winter to use as poles for their beans to climb. Baling twine was tied from one pole to the next for additional space for the vines to climb. The poles were saved from one year to the next. One summer chore was shelling beans, which meant separating the beans from the hull. I often did this under the tree with my grandfather.

These onions have had their tops woven and hung inside in a cool, dry place so they could be used over the winter months.

Sevin dust was the most popular pesticide, and often the plants looked snowy-white with the green plants covered with the white dust of the pesticide.[2]

Late summer and fall was the time for preparation of the food for use in the winter months. Many in the neighborhood canned (actually the canning process meant putting the food in jars) or froze many items such as corn. Certain root crops were stored for long periods, providing food for the winter. Onions were stored by weaving the tops and then hanging in a cool dark area; potatoes were stored by burying them under pine shats and dirt. When one wanted potatoes, they were dug up again for use. Sweet potatoes were stored in buildings where the temperature could be maintained at approximately 40 degrees. Sweet potatoes were not buried because the moisture would make them sprout.

Not every bounty from the garden was planted in the spring. Turnips are a fall/winter crop. Although turnip greens were sown in some gardens for both the turnips and the greens, the greens were often picked wild. It was

---

2. Organic pest control was also used. Dad used to laugh as he recounted how he responded to an ad for a guaranteed way to kill potato bugs. When the package arrived he opened it to find two wooden blocks, one marked "A" and the other"B". The instructions stated that one was to place the bug on block "A" and hit with block "B"

Rural Life in the 1950's and 60's

not uncommon to see families parked along the roadside, picking wild turnip greens in fallow fields. This was reflective of times in which all resources were used and little went to waste.

Lima (pole) beans at the end of season. This picture shows how they have not only climbed the posts but also the string criss crossed between the poles. Photo by the author courtesy of Jimmie Truitt, Jr.

Modern Kitchen Utensils of the 1950's

From the left: Egg beater, grater, potato masher, Joseph's milk bottle (it was delivered), flour sifter, rolling pin, and can opener. Photo by Tom and Teresa Adams.

Meals & Traditional Food

Mom was a good cook and our food was delicious; however, it would not be considered "heart-healthy" by today's standards. Breakfast often consisted of eggs and either bacon, scrapple, or sausage. When I first had eggs in a restaurant, I was surprised by the lack of taste. It was because Mom cooked our eggs with bacon grease. After breakfast, the grease went into a container on the stove for use at a later time. All hot breakfast foods were fried in a cast iron skillet...there were no non-stick pans at that time. Our milk was whole milk- not 2% or skim.

We had breakfast and all other meals at the kitchen table. We ate as a family unless a special event prevented it. We did not watch TV while eating; nor did we eat on TV trays. We usually did have the radio on in the morning during breakfast for the weather and school closings. All meals started by Dad asking the "Blessing" or as locally referred, "saying Grace."

We always referred to our midday meal as lunch. Many of the older farm families referred to it as "dinner." Usually, the families that referred to it as dinner were those families that had their largest meal of the day at noon. Until I was in the Seventh Grade, we had a traditional lunch— soup or sandwiches. In the summer, we always had sliced tomatoes and possibly cucumbers and vinegar as side dishes.

Mom's baking utensils included the flour sifter to remove lumps from the flour, the rolling pin to roll the dough for dumpin's or biscuits, and the egg beater to whip eggs to a fine consistency. Photo by Tom Adams.

Opening cans was a chore. The lid was punctured with the point of the opener and then sawed open with a seesaw motion leaving a sharp jagged edge. Potatoes were not instant but peeled and then mashed with the "masher" above for nearly every supper. Plenty of elbow grease was required. Photo by the author.

When I was in the Seventh Grade, we started having our largest meal of the day at noon, even though we still used the term lunch instead of dinner. There were two reasons for this. First, we used prison labor[1] on the farm and Dad found that by providing a good home cooked meal at noon, the workers were more loyal and were willing to work harder. Second, we were working hard on the farm and needed the big meal then and a lighter meal at the end of the day, because we went to bed early.

When the main meal was at noon, it could consist of hotdogs or hamburgers in steamed rolls, homemade soups, fried chicken, sandwiches, and when vegetables were in season it could include corn on the cob, sliced tomatoes, cucumbers in vinegar, lima beans, dried lima beans, asparagus soup, or fried squash.[2]

The evening meal might consist of fried pork chops, fried steak, fried fish, or fried chicken. As you may note, broiled was not on the menu. I did not have a broiled or barbecued steak until I was in college.

When we had lima beans, often referred to as butter beans, it was not as a side dish but as a main course. Mom always cooked a large pot, which lasted for several meals. The seasoning was provided by a large slab of fat meat. The same was true with dried limas in the fall and winter. Our sides were fresh, sliced tomatoes, corn on the cob and homemade biscuits. We drank copious amounts of sweet ice tea in the summer which Mom made by the pot full.

Other foods had traditional or standard sides. When we had fish, we always had turnip greens and cornbread. It was Mom's opinion that fish always tasted better on a rainy day. We usually got our fish from a door to door salesman. This salesman was normally someone known to my parents who had caught more fish than he could use. These people filled the trunks of their cars with ice and had the fish in the ice. They had portable scales that they hung on the trunk lid

---

1. Dad went to the prison each morning and picked up prisoners(referred to as trustees) to work on the farm. It cost $5.00 per day per prisoner and we provided their lunch. The prisoner got to keep $1.00 per day for their labor.
2. Certain foods were referred to as "messes". A mess consisted of enough for a meal, e.g., a mess of beans or a mess of greens.

to weigh the fish. They did not clean the fish. Mom would scale, gut, and behead the fish. I never had filleted fish until I was an adult.

In the late summer, Mom made cabbage, again seasoned with a slab of fat meat. Her asparagus soup in the spring was made with asparagus, diced potatoes, and drop dumplings, again seasoned with a slab of fat meat.

Sunday meal usually consisted of either chicken or beef and dumplings (pronounced dumplin's). Mom cooked carrots, halved potatoes and whole onions with the beef. When she had chicken and dumplings, it was important to have a fat, old hen which provided lots of good yellow (pronounced "yellar" by some) gravy for the dumplings.[3]

Mom and Dad occasionally ate boiled pig's feet. None of us kids touched them, so Mom always had something else for us to eat. One neighbor looked forward to an annual meal with a friend in which sow's-ear and pig tail topped the menu. Still others had frog legs, though they never made it onto our menu.

It seemed the smell of cooking lingered all day as mom prepared our meals. Many of her utensiles would seem old fashioned today. In addition to the cast iron skillets, she used hand egg-beaters, potato mashers, and flour sifters, instead of electric mixers and blenders.

It was not uncommon to have leftovers. Certain dishes were specifically made to last for several meals - such as beans, asaparagus soup, and vegetable beef soup. Other foods were resurrected in a different format, such as mashed potatoes. When they were left over, Mom often made potato cakes the next morning. They were made into patties and fried for breakfast.

We rarely had snacks. In season, we might have an oyster stew before bed. Occasionally, we had ice cream before bed. It was extremely rare to have pretzels or potato chips in the evening.

Our ice cream freezer was put to use in the summer. Mom mixed the ingredients and Dad and one or more of us kids turned the crank to churn and freeze the ice cream. Photo by the author.

One special treat in the summer was making home-made ice cream. We usually made either vanilla or chocolate but also made banana-flavored on more than one occasion. The wooden ice cream freezer was filled with ice around the metal container holding the ingredients. Then Dad or Merrill, or in later years, I would crank the freezer while someone sat on it. It seemed to take a long time but was definitely worth the effort.

---
3. See Appendix A for some of Mom's recipes

From the early days of Grotto Pizza in Rehoboth Beach. The sign at the top reads "Pizza Pies" Photo courtesy of Grotto's Pizza.

We did not have ethnic foods. No one ate Chinese food; in fact, we did not eat rice. Mashed potatoes provided the starch for nearly every meal. Our ventures into Italian cuisine were the spaghetti meals Mom cooked in the frying pan with the sauce.

I was very young when I first heard of pizza. Ronald came home and mentioned that someone was giving away samples of pizza pie on the boardwalk in Rehoboth. This person was Dominick Pulieri, owner of Grotto Pizza (locally known as Grottos). No one locally knew what pizza was. By the mid-1960s, Grottos was the place to be for all teens.

Although pizza and other ethnic foods did become acceptable and a treat for the teens, like most of the rural families around us, we stuck to a meat and potatoes fare.

Dominick Pulieri stretching dough at one of his Rehoboth Beach Grottos Restaurants. Grottos started as a takeout stand on Rehoboth Avenue and now has 21 locations throughout Delaware and Pennsylvania. Photo courtesy of Grottos Pizza

Rural Life in the 1950's and 60's

Home Visits

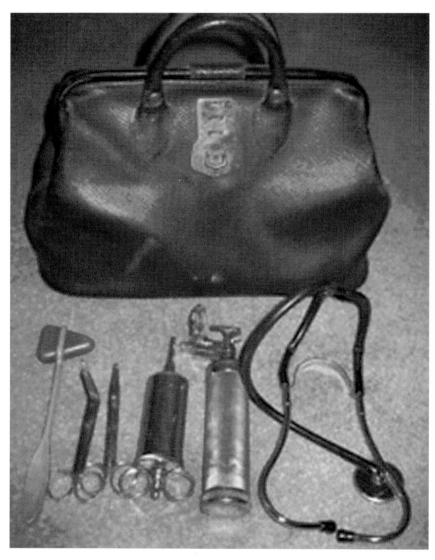

Doctors made home visits and brought a bag of instruments and some medicines.

Medical

Much of our medical care was through home remedies....one did not go to a doctor unless one was really sick or hurt. If one had a sore throat, one was to gargle with warm salt water. If one had an earache, a hot-water bottle was placed next to the ear, although some believed blowing smoke from a cigarette was the cure.

I was fortunate to have been born after the Castor Oil period. My brothers were often given, as were others in the neighborhood, Castor Oil at the first sign of any illness. It has been described to me as the nastiest concoction ever made.

If one had nasal congestion, known as being "stopped up," Vicks Vapor Rub was placed on the nose. If one had chest congestion, Vicks was applied to the chest. Indigestion was cured by drinking a half glass of water mixed with a 1/2 teaspoon of baking soda. Bee stings were treated by placing a paste—made from baking soda and vinegar—directly on the sting. Everyone kept epsom salts for sprains. Although I never had a poultice, many used a potato plaster or poultice for boils and chest colds. My mother often referred to having taken sugar with a drop of coal oil for sore throats and colds. There were still plenty of "Patent Medicines" in use, and the drugstore shelves were filled with such concoctions.[1]

Even though the neighborhood consisted of teetotallers, it was not uncommon for some of the old-timers to have some whiskey in a cabinet for "medicinal" purposes. I was with one neighbor when she thought she was suffering a heart attack. We called the doctor, and while waiting, she asked that I get some whiskey from the cabinet. I then helped hold

---

1. Patent medicines weren't actually patented for the most part but were actually trademarked. The one that was actually patented was Castoria, which Mom thought was a cure-all. Patent medicines are associated with those 18th and 19th elixers and cure alls marketed under such names as Mugwomp or Swamp Root, etc. Many refer to them as "Snake Oil." They were often vegetable extracts laced with alcohol.

her up as she took a sip and then had me put it away with the admonishment that it was for "medicinal purposes" only.

I often heard the names of Doc Waples, Dr. Van, and old-man Doc Smoot. Doc Smoot was called "old-man" because his son joined the practice. Doc Waples had been the doctor for my brothers. He was known for giving two types of pills—a black creosote pill or a pink pill. One other unique feature of medical care then was that the doctors came to the patients. House calls were the norm, not the exception.

Our doctor was Dr. Smoot (the son), who had set up practice with Dr. Wildberger. Dr. Wildberger became our family doctor when Dr. Smoot left to continue his education to become an eyes, ear, nose and throat specialist. Dr. Wildberger was a true pillar of our community. He loved sports and attended all Georgetown athletic events and even gave free physicals to all the athletes.[2]

Dr. Wildberger enjoying his favorite pastime....watching the local football team. Picture courtesy of Lorraine Wildberger Cooper.

The County did have three hospitals that served its residents: Milford Memorial in Milford, Beebe in Lewes, and Nanticoke in Seaford. Hospitals were reserved for serious matters like broken bones, heart attacks, cancer, and surgeries. We did not go to the emergency room for routine care. In fact, as noted above, we didn't even go to the doctor for routine care; we used home remedies.

One can't discuss medical issues in this era without discussing the polio epidemic. Nearly everyone knew someone inflicted with this dreaded disease. Many were lucky and were able to walk with braces and crutches or maybe with just a limp. Others were not so lucky. My aunt Margaret, nee Conaway, married to my Uncle Charles Moore, was stricken when my cousin, Lynn, was just 10 months old. She had extended stays in the hospital and in the iron lung. Only her head was visible while she was in this machine that kept her breathing.

---

2. There is a scholarship set up in his memory. Contributions can be sent to the attention of the Guidance Counselor at Sussex Central High School.

Rural Life in the 1950's and 60's

She was released to come home but was confined to a rocking bed to assist her circulation for the rest of her life. Throughout her tribulations, she never complained and her many visitors commented that they were uplifted by her ever-present smile.

The March of Dimes was a nation wide fund raising effort to help eradicate polio. Fundraising drives occurred every year in the school and community. Polio shots were mandated by the schools and were given in the schools. Fortunately, this disease is just a bad memory today.

There were two dentists in town, Dr. Cannon and Dr. Reese Swain. Our dentist was Reese Swain, and to say he was a character would be an understatement. He loved to hunt and play the horses. His office was on the second floor of the Thompson building which, when I first started seeing him, was located on Cherry Lane behind the Courthouse. To get to his office, one climbed a set of steep, narrow stairs that added to the trepidation of a young patient. He was an imposing man and also provided dental care for the prison. By that, I mean he pulled their teeth. There was no high tech care. Some times, when I went for an appointment, prisoners were in the waiting room, with a guard. I often heard a yell as he pulled the tooth of the prisoner in the chair while the others looked very squeamish as they waited their turn.

On another occasion, I went with my Pop Pop Wilson, another character in his own right, to have his tooth pulled. When Reese gave him the Novocaine, he started yelling "get that horse needle out of my mouth." Another elementary student a year older than I, who was waiting his turn to be treated, became afraid and started crying. After that, I never had Novocaine from him. I had teeth filled and even a pulp cap on one of my front teeth, but I would rather face the pain than that "horse needle."

We also had two drugstores (they were not called Pharmacies) in town. The traditional drugstore was on the northeast corner of Race and East Market Streets, which is now a pawn shop. It was operated by Warren Edinger until he sold it to Robert L Snively in the 60's.[3]

I worked for Mr. Snively soon after he purchased the drugstore. Many came into the store for medical advice and referred to him as doctor. The store was full of patent medicines, and he filled the prescriptions and placed them in vials with labels that he typed himself with the hunt and peck method

Signs such as these dotted small town America. They represeenteed the Rexall drugstores that were locally owned in each community.

---

3. I was Mr. Snively's first new employee. I worked as a clerk at age 16 for 90 cents per hour.

and capped them in pre-tamper proof tops. Mr. Snively worked very long hours and did not have an assistant to help if he were not there. The store was closed on Wednesday afternoons in the tradition of the town.

The other drugstore was opened on Route 113 next to Dr. Smoot's and Dr. Wildberger's office. It was owned by Landis Wilson, uncle to our former mayor, Ed Lambden. Mr. Wilson had previously owned the drugstore in town and was the person that sold it to Mr. Edinger. The rumor was that there was a non-compete clause that prevented him from opening a new drugstore in Georgetown. At that time, Georgetown had not expanded beyond its traditional circle shape, and the property on Route 113 was outside of town limits. Unlike the drugstore in town, he had a soda fountain. To encourage business, he gave coupons for a free ice cream cone to all patients of the local doctors. Although it did not stay open very long, it did leave a big impact on a small-town rumor mill.

The drug store in Georgetown at the corner of Race and Market Streets. The 5 and Dime was next door. At the times, most stores had awnings that were lowered during the day to keep the stores cool. Photo courtesy of Delaware Public Archives.

Beebe Hospital in Lewes in the 1950s. Photo courtesy of Delaware Digital Postcard Collection, University of Delaware Library, Newark, Delaware.

Rural Life in the 1950's and 60's

Telephone Operators

In the 1950's and 1960's long distance, information, and emergency calls were made with the assistance of operators. The central switchboard office was in Georgetown. Photo courtesy of Delaware Public Archives.

Telephone

There were no cell phones, cordless phones or touch tone phones. Likewise, there were no call-waiting or multi-function

The basic black rotary dial phone like the one I first remember. It was hard wired to the wall so it wasn't portable beyond the length of its cord. Photo by the author.

phones. Our phones were basic black, rotary, dial phones.

Our phone lines were not "private." We had a "party line," which meant some of our neighbors shared our line and could pick their phones up and listen to our conversations. Each party on the "party line" had a different ring—one long ring was for one family, two short rings, & three short rings still another and another. It was not uncommon to hear a click while on the phone, which indicated someone else on the party line had picked up the line. If they were merely checking to see if the line was open so they could make a call, they quickly hung up, making another clicking sound. If the second click was not heard, one knew the other party was listening in for entertainment,

This is the basic black rotary dial wall phone like we had for many years. It too was hard-wired and could not be moved from location to location. Photo by the author.

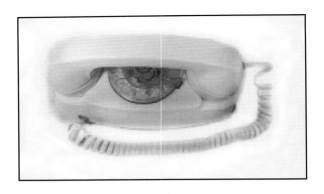

The princess phone was the first phone I remember in a color other than black and the first phone that we plugged into a jack. An additional feature was a lighted rotary dial. Photo by the author.

so they were often told "to hang up and quit listening."

There were no area codes—just the four digit numbers. Our number was 2871. Anyone in the Georgetown area simply dialed that without any other numbers. Local exchanges, e.g., 856 for Georgetown, did not come to the area until April 15, 1962. Area Codes came into use shortly thereafter.

One could not go to a store and buy a phone, the phones were actually owned by the telephone company, and a rental fee was added to the bill. If one wanted a new phone, one had to go to the phone company business office and get the new phone.

It was not until my high school years that the public was given the option to upgrade from the basic black to a "Princess" rotary dial phone. At that time, I saw my first phone jacks that allowed a phone to be unplugged and moved to another location that had a jack. Prior to that, phones were hard wired and could not be moved.

Long distance calls were made with the help of the operator. The operators worked in the office on Race Street in Georgetown. The business office was located several blocks away on East Market Street.

The phone company provided summer jobs for many students as operators. Many also worked for the phone company as repairmen and linemen. There were no underground cables back then, and poles and overhead wires went to every home that had service. The linemen did not have bucket trucks, but instead, climbed the poles with climbing spikes strapped to their feet and

There were no bucket trucks to lift linemen to their work. Instead, they usually relied on climbing spikes strapped to their legs and a climbing belt. When they reached their work site, they firmly stuck their spikes in the pole and leaned back against the belt to free their hands for worik. Photo courtesy of Jim Bowden

Rural Life in the 1950's and 60's

legs. They then worked for long periods of time strapped to the pole by their safety belt.

Not everyone had the luxury of a phone in their home. To make a call, they either went to a neighbor's or friend's house or used a phone booth. There were several styles of phone booth. Some were primarily for outdoor use as the one pictured in this chapter, and others were for indoor use. They were usually made of wood frame to fit an interior decor. Many movie scenes showed long lines of phone booths in the lobbies of large hotels. With the advent of cell phones today, not only is the phone booth rapidly becoming a thing of the past but also the land line phone.

The pay phone booth is now a thing of the past with the advent of cell phones. In my youth, they were conveniently placed so traveling members of the public and those without phones had access. Photo by the author

WJWL

WJWL was the AM station on Route 113 north of Georgetown. In the late 1960's, it acquired a sister station, WSEA-FM. Photo courtesy of Delaware Public Archives.

Radio

We had an AM radio—no FM and no digital dials. It was an old, brown radio that received our most important station, WJWL, or, as their jingle stated, "9-0 on your radio." Bob Smith was the long time radio announcer. We listened for the local news, school closings, music programs, and local interest programs. Ed Marzoa hosted the first call-in show and Sam Wilson, one of our current county councilmen, was a frequent caller.

One special and important feature was the Poultry Auction held shortly before noon. It was the actual auction, broadcast live from Selbyville, in which poultry buyers from around the country bid on actual chicken flocks. Dad always listened so that he could follow the prices being paid for chickens.

The chicken auction was broadcast live every weekday on WJWL. Please note the list of approved buyers and the microphones for both WBOC and WJWL radio. The chalk board to the right listed the names of the farms for the flocks being sold. The auctioneer was Carroll Long. Photo courtesy of the Delaware Agricultural Musuem and Village.

Saturdays featured the Ralph Hoebee Show. Ralph, the self proclaimed "Troubadour of the Eastern Shore", was a house painter from Milton who performed his show live 90 per cent of the time, and when unable to do so he taped his 15-minute show in his home. His show started with him singing his theme song "In the cottage small where the pines grow tall..." He played guitar, sang, and played harmonica. He also read his own commercials—one sponsor I remember was Bob Willey & Sons in Milton. He had a band (but not on the show) named Ralph Hoebee and the Indian River Boys. He played many benefits. If he heard of someone injured or sick and they needed financial help, he would announce a benefit on the show to raise money for them. He would then perform for no charge to help.

Ralph Hoebee, the" Troubadour of the Eastern Shore" as he appeared at WJWL, 90 on the Radio in Georgetown, Delaware. His show was a staple of Saturday morning for many years. In addition to his show he often appeared with his "Indian River Boys" to benefit the sick and needy with no pay for his efforts. Photo courtesy of John Hoebee.

Years later, when in college, I played in a rock band with his son, John, who was a very good singer and guitar player in his own right. It was then that I met Ralph Hoebee. He was a nice man who did his best to entertain and to help others.

In the late 1960s', WJWL acquired a sister station, WSEA-FM. It was primarily a rock station and a favorite of many students at the new college in Georgetown.

Although many towns had stations, their range was limited, which created a lot of static. We no longer have the small stations in each town. Due to improved technology, stations can broadcast over a long distance and have been consolidating.

The first super station to us was WABC in New York, and the favorite show of many teens was "Cousin Brucie." This is the same Cousin Brucie who hosts a show today on the "60s on 6" channel on Sirius Radio. We were unable to receive the old WABC program on the radio in our house, but it came in loud and clear on the car radio.

Portable radios were not common at that time. The first portable radios were approximately three inches wide, six inches long, and one inch thick. They were often referred to as Japanese or transistor radios.

The younger families tended to have newer plastic cabinet radios but the woodeen desktop style and even wooden floor cabinet models were still in use by some of the older families. Photo by the author.

Frankly, many considered them to be junk. The reception was very poor and they were AM only.

There were actually more of the old, large radios still in use than the portables. The old, large ones were often floor models that were in wooden cabinets. These were often placed near a window for better reception and had a wire running out the window to a pipe to act as a ground.

The old timers often talked of gathering around the radio in the evenings and listening to the serials like "Amos and Andy" or "The Lone Ranger." Many of my generation heard from our parents about the fireside chats by President Franklin Roosevelt during the Great Depression and World War II.

My Uncle Cartlton remembers my grandfather owning the first radio in the neighborhood. Prize fights brought the entire neighborhood over to visit. He said the women came inside to visit as the men stayed outside next to the open windows to listen to the fight.

Another picture of the poultry auction. Here chickens are being displayed in a chicken coop. Photo courtesy of Delaware Agricultural Museum and Village.

THE SUSSEX COUNTIAN

The *Sussex Countian* contained all the local news and gossip The *Countian* was started as *The Sussex Republican* by Robert G Houston in 1893. From the author's collection.

Newspapers

Our local newspapers were *The Sussex Countian*, published in Georgetown, which was received in the mail on Thursdays and *The Milford Chronicle*, published appropriately in Milford, which was received in the mail on Fridays. Many of the small towns had their own weeklies.

There were also larger newspapers that covered downstate. *The Morning News* and *The Evening Journal* were the only true state-wide papers. *The Delaware State News* and *The Salisbury Times* were regional papers that covered downstate with the Salisbury Times being more of interest to those in the south western areas of the County.

The *Countian* was full of local information, sports, births, marriages, deaths, and news of local interest. All the local communities in the distribution area had "socials" that gave the comings and goings of the locals. This included birthday celebrations, visits, and other information that was only of interest to those involved.[1]

The main interest in the *Chronicle* in our home was for the advertising and public auction notices. Dad attended a lot of farm and antique auctions and there was a far better listing in the *Chronicle*. This was before the advent of *The Sussex Guide* as we now know it.

The *Guide* started in 1959 and did not have the pages and pages of classifieds that it does now. In fact, I have a 1964 issue that has only one page, front and back, of classified ads. Now this free weekly publication is known for its classified ads, auction notices, and car dealer and realtor listing ads.

---

1. While in law school, one of my classmates read my paper and saw the Georgetown Socials and exclaimed "you must be a real deal back home, it's in the socials that you went home for the weekend and listed everyone you saw while there." Little did he know that trivia such as that was the norm for that column.

The Sussex Guide truly was and is everywhere in Sussex County. When it was first published, the covers often contained historic photos of the area. I used to collect them for use in my 4th grade Delaware history course. Photo by the author courtesy of Clarke White.

There were two daily newspapers in the time frame discussed in this book owned by the News-Journal Co., a wholly owned subsidiary of Christina Securities, the holding company for Du Pont Co. stock. They were the Morning News and the Evening Journal which were both published 6 days a week until 1975 at which time the Sunday News Journal was added. This office was located on the Circle next to the Brick Hotel. In the 1960's, the paper had a large presence in Sussex due to the aggressive reporting by its bureau chief, Ron Williams. It was appropriate that the paper had a large presence in Sussex, since one of the predecessor papers was the Every Evening founded by Georgetown native Willam T. Crossdale. Photo courtesy of Delaware Public Archives.

Rural Life in the 1950's and 60's

THURSDAY, JUNE 25, 1970

Georgetown Socials

Mr. Elwood Johnson of St. Johns is a patient in the Peninsula General Hospital, Salisbury, Md., Room 222.

Mr. and Mrs. Watson Cook and granddaughter, Kim Williams, and Mr. and Mrs. William Cook and daughters were the week-end guests of their son-in-law and daughter, Mr. and Mrs. ___

Capt. and Mrs. William Jones and Mr. and Mrs. William Stevenson were in Newark last week-end where they attended the VFW Convention.

Mr. and Mrs. Harry Coar and family and Mrs. Nelson Coar spent a day last week in Ocean City, N. J.

Mr. and Mrs. Howard Brock and family are on a two weeks' vacation trip to Tennessee where they are visiting relatives.

Lance Keeler, young son of Mr. and Mrs. Eddie Keeler, is a patient in Milford Memorial Hospital where he underwent surgery.

Mr. and Mrs. Guy White of Federalsburg spent Tuesday with Mrs. Helen Truitt.

Mr. J. Everett Moore, Jr. entertained the incoming and the outgoing members of the Student Government Association of the DT&CC at a barbeque at the home of his parents Saturday evening.

Mr. and Mrs. Floyd Megee, Jr. and family, Mr. and Mrs. Edward Dorey and family and Mr. and Mrs. Tim Wilkerson and family of Millsboro spent last week camping at Cherry Stone Camping Ground in Virginia.

Mr. and Mrs. Ralph Prettyman and family are spending the summer at Rehoboth Beach.

Cecelia Godwin entertained her friends Saturday at a birthday party at the home of her parents, Mr. and Mrs. William Godwin.

Mrs. Raymond A. Rust entertained the members of her bridge club Tuesday evening.

Mr. Dale Mears returned home on Monday from Delaware Hospital after being a patient there for four months.

William Kirk Lawson, son of Mr. and Mrs. William Lawson, was baptised on Sunday at Bethesda Methodist Church. Attending the services were the godparents, Mr. and Mrs. Jeff Carmine of Milford and Mr. and Mrs. Dale R. Pepper, Jr.

Mr. and Mrs. Rodney W. Wilgus, Jr. and daughter, Janelle, of Hawaii and Chief (USCG) Wesley G. Fulcher and Mrs. Fulcher and children, Kathy Sue and Rodney, of Newport,

THURSDAY, DECEMBER 9, 1971

Georgetown Socials

Mrs. Preston Johnson is a patient in Beebe Hospital, Lewes.

* * *

Mr. and Mrs. Everett Moore had as their guests for dinner on Thanksgiving Day J. Everett Moore, Jr. of the University of Delaware, Mr. and Mrs. Larry W. Moore, Mr. and Mrs. Carlton R. Moore and family, Mr. and Mrs. Ronald W. Moore and son, Mr. and Mrs. Merrill C. Moore and Mr. Carroll Wilson.

* * *

S/Sgt. and Mrs. Ronald T. Wilson and daughters, Diane, Donna & Dana of Fort Bragg, N. C., spent the holidays with Mr. and Mrs. Marshall Wilson. Monday, Sgt. Wilson left by plane for Indianapolis, Indiana, where he will attend Recruiting school. He was accompanied to the Philadelphia Airport by Mr. and Mrs. James Wilson and Mrs. Inge Wilson and daughter, Dana.

* * *

Mrs. Clara Jewell and Mrs. Mary Spicer have returned home from a vacation in Orlando, Florida.

* * *

The employees of the Sussex County Court House held their Christmas Luncheon Tuesday at Jones Memorial Hall.

* * *

Mrs. Martha Betts is a patient in Milford Memorial Hospital.

* * *

Mr. and Mrs. James Owen and daughter, Susan, of Newark were the week-end guests of Mr. and Mrs. James Marvel and Mr. and Mrs. Fred Sammons.

* * *

Miss Teresa Moore celebrated her 17th birthday November 24 at the home of her parents, Mr. and Mrs. Everett Moore. Guests were members of the family.

WBOC TV PARK

WBOC-TV PARK as it appeared in the 1950's and 1960's. It is located on Route 13 northbound, just south of Salisbury, Maryland. Photo courtesy of WBOC-TV

Television

My earliest memories of the TV were of our family sitting together watching shows like The Ed Sullivan Show, Jack Benny, Jackie Gleason in The Honeymooners, Lawrence Welk, Bonanza, and Gunsmoke. Children's shows were "The Howdy Doody Show," "Rin Tin Tin," "The Pinky Lee Show," "Ding Dong School," "Roy Rogers Show," "Sky King," and "My Friend Flicka." At that time there were very few cartoons.

There were no cable TV or satellite dishes of any sort. Everyone used outside antennas, which were either mounted on the roof or on a pole near the house. The picture was very "snowy" for lack of reception and the vertical and horizontal holds needed adjustment constantly. If the T.V. needed repair, a repairman came to the house with a large specialized tool box that held lots of vacuum tubes. There were no transistors or similar electronics at the time. Because there were tubes, it took time for the tubes to warm up after the TV was turned on. The TVs were black and white. I knew of no one that owned a color TV.

One feature that I rarely see today is the "sign on" and "sign off" the air. A short religious message and the national anthem were played before the station went off the air for the evening. There were no 24-hour stations at that time. A test pattern then remained on the screen throughout the night.

My brother, Merrill, in December, 1956. Please note the rounded screen TV with the antenna rotor box on top the TV. It was used to turn the antenna toward the station one was watching in hopes of getting better reception. Photo from author's collection.

The TV repairman always brought his toolbox full of tubes. Nearly every repair job entailed replacing tubes. TVs and radios did not start up as soon as one turned them on but took time to warm up. Photo by the author.

The same was repeated in the morning before signing back on the air.

Initially, our shows came from the Baltimore, Philadelphia and Washington, DC stations. In Sussex, we tended to get better reception from the Baltimore stations, thus creating many Colts and Oriole fans in the area. I remember the Eastern Shore as being referred to "As The Land Of Pleasant Living" on the Baltimore station. I believe it was part of a beer commercial, and I remember it being repeated by Chuck Thompson on the Orioles' broadcasts. The NBC affiliate from Baltimore was often the clearest channel, so the national news that many of us watched was the "The Huntley-Brinkley Report" with David Brinkley and Chet Huntley. It was only on for 15 minutes, and the "Good Night, David" and "Good Night, Chet" sign-off they used at the end of each telecast was known to all.

When I refer to the "clearest" channel, it is a relative term. Even then the picture faded in and out and was difficult to see. Most roof-top antennae had rotors attached which allowed the antenna to be pointed in the direction of the station. Often, the channel was clear at the start of the program but became snowy during the show. We jumped to the control box to move the antenna while others in the room let us know if it was clear.

WBOC 16 in Salisbury went on the air on July 15, 1954, and became the first broadcast station on the peninsula. After a few years, it became the favored channel because of the clearer reception and its local news and weather. John B. Greenberger was the news anchor and general go-to guy at the station.

There were lots of local programming, which often was in 15-minute segments. That was especially so of some of the local religious shows. One such show that was

In the days before the 24 hour news cycle we watched the 15 minute nightly Huntley-Brinkley Report

Rural Life in the 1950's and 60's

Election night coverage in the early 1960s. There were no huge sets, computer graphics, and expert commentators. Just a single metal desk and two telephones. Photo courtesy of WBOC TV.

It was at that time that we started watching Walter Cronkite with his familiar sign-off "And that's the way it is" at the end of each telecast with his baritone voice. Many of my generation remember his emotional broadcast of the events surrounding the assassination of President Kennedy.

John B. Greenberger was the newsman, announcer, and general go to guy at WBOC in the 1950s. Photo courtesy of WBOC TV.

popular in the neighborhood was the Evangel Hour with Rev. Ray Chamberlain from Salisbury, Maryland. He gave a sermon and scripture reading, had his wife read a poem, and then they sang a duet. He then read the names of some shut-ins and prayed for their well being. It was a very popular show.

Although primarily a CBS affiliate, WBOC did have popular shows from the other three networks, ABC, NBC, and DuMont, as well. There was little reason to watch the other stations with poor signals.

Walter Cronkite reporting on the assassination of President Kennedy. He was often referred to as the most trusted man in America and was known for his reporting of the Vietnam War and the space missions.

Years later, when I attended one of the national political conventions, I had an opportunity to see and stand next to him. I was surprised that he was not a tall man, as I had believed from seeing him on TV and imagined from his booming, authoritative voice.

Here is Huntley and Brinkley during the coverage of the 1952 Republican Convention. Please notice one telephone on the desk between them.

There were no satellite or cable TV at the time and bunny ears were ineffective in rural areas. Homes had antennae placed on either the roof or on a tall pole near the home in order to pick up the far away signals. Photo by the author.

An interior view of the WBOC reception area. Note the rounded TV screen and the ash tray which was a staple in all offices and waiting rooms of the era. Photo courtesy of WBOC TV.

Rural Life in the 1950's and 60's

Rural Delivery

Our mail was delivered to our mailbox on the side of the road. When we had outgoing mail we raised the flag as shown above. That resulted in the mailman stopping to our box even if he had no mail to deliver. Photo by the author.

Mail

We received our mail from a mailman who drove from house to house. We were part of the Rural Free Delivery (RFD) system. Although our mail should have been addressed RFD#5, often it would be shortened to "RD," "RR," or "Route." Because we were such a small, static population, everyone knew everyone. We even received mail as "near

This letter was addressed to my brothers and me simply as Route 5 with no box number nor reference to our parents. From the authors collection.

St. John's," "near Georgetown," or "RR, Georgetown." I am unaware of anyone in the neighborhood who had a post office box. We also sent our mail through the mailman.

If we had outgoing mail, we simply put up the flag on the side of the mailbox to let the mailman know there was outgoing mail to pick up from the box. If we needed stamps, we put the correct amount of change in the box with a note, and the stamps were left in the mailbox. Therefore, there was no reason to go to the post office.

There were no UPS or Fed Ex or other overnight delivery services that I am aware of. The only option for speedier delivery was air mail. Air mail envelopes were made of a lighter paper and had red markings around the edge.

Our fast mail was airmail. It was more expensive, and because of that, airmail envelopes and stationery were made from onion-skin paper to keep the weight and thus the expense down. From the author's collection

The correct designation on rural mail was RFD for Rural Free Delivery. Even though we had a box number, we still received mail without it being included. From the author's collection.

Often RFD was shortened to just "RD." Again, note that the box number is not included. From the author's collection.

The Georgetown Post Office located on the Circle. This building is now part of the county complex housing County Council Chambers. Please note the wooden, directional sign-post to the right, the mail box in the front and the Army Recruiting sign. Photo from the author's collection.

Rural Life in the 1950's and 60's

Transportation

Dad with our family's new 1955 Buick. The five-year-old author is standing at the back of the vehicle. Our family always bought Buicks. We had a 1950 prior to this one, and the Buick shown above was replaced by a 1960 Buick LeSabre.

Transportation

Although I am not a product of the horse and buggy era, I do remember one person, Woody Stewart, riding his horse and buggy to Church. He tied it up under the tree at Wilson's Store.

It was a time of transition. My father's generation grew up with horse and buggy and the start of the auto industry. Our roads reflected this transition. Many of our roads were not paved but were dirt. Peterkin's Road, Deep Branch Road, Hollis Road, Anderson Corner Road, Doddtown Road, Pie Road, Rust Road, Simpler Branch Road, and parts of Industrial Park Boulevard (the part from Springfield Road north to Route 9) to name a few, were all dirt. Senator Curt Steen of Dagsboro, Delaware, was the go to person if one wanted their road paved. Although I am sure other senators and representatives and the powerful Delaware State Highway Commission members also had roads paved, Senator Steen is the name I remember as being synonymous with the paving.

Many dual highways that we know today were single lane highways at that time. Route 113 from Milford south was not a dual highway until my high school years. Route 1 south from Milford was a single lane highway and was referred to as Route 14. It actually had a drawbridge across the Broadkill River.

This is a 1948 Hudson similar to the first car I remember of my grandfather Wilson. In 1954, Hudson and Nash-Kelvinator merged to create the American Motor Company which produced the Rambler.

There were many makes of cars that are no longer made: DeSoto, Kaiser, Pontiac, and Oldsmobile, among others. I remember my grandfather's Hudson car— I remember two, my brother Ronald's Studebakers I remember three—1951, 1953, and 1960—and one friend's Rambler and another's Corvair.

Most towns had at least one car dealership. Georgetown had several. The Studebaker dealership, known as Sussex Studebaker Co., was co-owned by Elwood (Woody) Steele, who lived in the neighborhood and attended St. John's. That dealership is now Terry Megee's "Megee Motors." His father, Floyd, was co-owner with Woody. The Plymouth dealership, Conaway Motors, was located on the circle where the Family Court now sits. Burton's Chevrolet was on East Market Street next to Henry's Newsstand, and the Buick Dealership, was also on East Market Street where Givens Flowers and

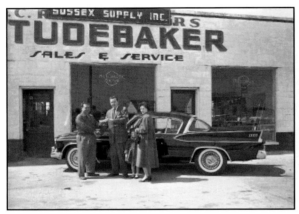

A salesman and customers with a new Studebaker at Sussex Motors in Georgetown, which was owned by Floyd Megee, Sr. and Elwood (Woody) Steele. It was previously known as Rust Bothers, and now it is known as Megee Motors owned by Terry Megee. Photo courtesy of Delaware Public Archives

Gifts is now. When Harry Smith bought the Buick dealership he built a new building on Route 113. It is now occupied by Delaware Camping Center, Inc. The Pontiac dealership was owned by the Abbott family and was located on North Bedford Street just south of Megee Motors. The Rambler dealership was owned by Lee Kersey and was located on Rt 113 in Millsboro.

Vehicles had one of three types of license tags: numbers only for passenger cars, C and then numbers for commercial vehicles, including pick ups, and P/C, meaning "passenger/commercial," which was on many station wagons. At that time, Delaware did not have its cabinet form of government and was run by boards and commissions. The Highway Commission was very powerful and contained many prominent Sussex

This is typical of the style of gas pumps in the 1950s. In addition to American, Texico Fire Chief, and the brands we have today, there was ESSO, the predeceasor to EXXON. Its slogan was "Put a tiger in your tank." Photo by the author.

Rural Life in the 1950's and 60's

Countians. As a result, many four-digit tags were distributed to their friends. These tags are highly prized and valuable today. They are valuable because in Delaware, unlike many states, one keeps the same license plate from year to year. The tag is renewed by a dated sticker, which is affixed to the tag. The tags can be transferred from car to car and can be sold on the open market. Some low number tags have fetched as high as $500,000.00 at specialty auctions.

Just as is the case today, certain families bought certain cars. Our family always had Buicks, as did Uncle Charles. The Jimmie Truitt family was always loyal to Fords.

This is a Chevy Corvair. This is the car that launched the career of Ralph Nader as a consumer advocate. His book "Unsafe At Any Speed" about the Corvair marked the beginning of car safety standards.

Although my grandfather Wilson had a 1955 Chevy with an automatic transmission, it was a rarity. Most cars had three-speed standard transmissions with the shifter being on the steering column, not the floor. The cars had AM radio only if there was a radio at all. I was totally unaware of FM radio either in my cars or at home. We did not have air conditioning in the cars. The windows worked with hand crank...not power, and seat adjustments were made with levers. Nor did the cars have power steering or power brakes. The light-dimmer switch was on the floor, and the ignition was normally on the dash, not on the steering column.

This is a 1953 Studebaker like the one my brother, Ronald, owned. Its design was very sleek and futuristic for the time. Packard (a luxery car maker) bought out Studebaker in 1954 but continued to produce cars under the Studebaker name. Unfortunately, Studebakers went out of production in 1964 in the U.S.- although they did produce cars in Canada until 1966.

Most people, especially young people, worked on their own cars. This was before the days of solid-state ignition and on-board computers. Every service station and many of the small country stores sold spark plugs, oil, and fan belts. As teenagers, we learned how to set the gap in the plugs, set the points, change the oil, and how to trouble shoot car problems.

Sixteen-year-olds did not expect to get a car upon reaching driving age as they do now. Most would drive the family car, and their dates and other activities had to be coordinated with the family usage.

Although there were other modes of transportation, we often romanticize past rail usage. However, during my lifetime, there has not been any passenger train service in Sussex, and I do not remember knowing anyone that had traveled by train.

Growin' Up Country

A view from the south side of East Market Street Georgetown looking north showing pumps from 2 stations across the street from each other. Note the S & H Green Stamp sign. These were the traditional style stations in the 50s and 60s. Everything was full service which meant an attendant pumped the gas, checked the oil, fluids in the radiator, and checked the air pressure in the tires. There were still stations that served as a house for the owners family in the back and the front was a small station or store with gas pumps. Photo courtesy of Delaware Public Archives.

There were people in the neighborhood that traveled extensively across the country by bus. I had a great aunt that traveled throughout the west, visiting Indian Reservations. I had another relative who followed the Oral Roberts "Healing Tent Crusades" by bus. I had the opportunity to travel by bus in 1969 to Philadelphia to get a visa for a trip to Peru. The bus seemed to stop at every small town the entire length of the state. It was a slow way to travel.

In 1969, I did fly to Peru. That was my first experience on an airplane. I flew from Dulles, which at that time seemed stuck in the boonies miles and miles from any other building or activity. In those days, it was the norm to dress up to fly. I remember wearing a suit on the flight, and most other men either had a suit or sport coat.

It was my first flight and I was petrified. I sat next to two nuns. They were probably the first nuns that I was in close proximity to, and definitely the first I had ever spoken with. As a farm boy from Sussex, I was totally unfamiliar with the nuns' religion and its practices. When the wheels of the plane lifted after takeoff, I was apprehensive about the sound and vibration. The nuns made the sign of the cross, and I was positive that they were doing that in preparation for our impending death, and we were going to crash. When they realized my thoughts, they had a good laugh and assured me that was not the case.

It was while being in Peru that I witnessed another form of transportation: space travel. The Apollo 11 moon landing occurred while I was in Lima, Peru.

Conaway Motors was located on the Circle where the Family Court is now situated. It was one of five new-car dealerships in Georgetown. Photo courtesy of Delaware State Archives.

Rural Life in the 1950's and 60's

Jason School

Jason School opened in October of 1950 and closed in June of 1967, when public schools were integrated. This facility is now known as the Jason Building on the campus of Delaware Technical & Community College, Owens Campus, in Georgetown, Delaware. The school was named for William C. Jason, a prominent educator and theologian in the late 1800's and early 1900's. Photo from *The Pioneer, 1960*, courtesy of Dr. Reba Hollingsworth.

Segregation & Integration

African-Americans were known as "Colored People" or Negroes in polite society in the 1950's and early 1960's. That is the way they were referred to in our neighborhood. In fact, I'm not sure I even heard the "N" word prior to Junior. High School. It definitely was not a word allowed in our household.

We had a black woman who came once a week to help Mom with the cleaning, and Mom and Dad had a black tenant in a property they owned in town. Those were the only direct contacts I had with "colored people" until high school. There were no blacks in our neighborhood or Church.

Our school was segregated. The blacks attended small, local schools for their elementary education and then attended Jason High School in Georgetown[1]. That was the only black high school in the county. When integration occurred, Georgetown was the last segregated high school because

Dr. Wildberger and a nurse giving injections at one of the local "colored" elementary schools. Photo courtesy of Lorraine Cooper.

the blacks in Georgetown were allowed to continue their high school at Jason. Although blacks attended Georgetown High School when I was in high school, there were none in my grade until my senior year in 1968.

The first place I really became aware of segregation was at Trap Pond on the fourth of July. Blacks were not allowed on the same side of the pond as whites. Segregation also

---

1. Jason High School became the Southern branch of Delaware Technical and Community College in 1967 after it closed due to integration. The original building of the college is named the "Jason Building".

occurred in the movie theater. Blacks had to sit in the balcony. Both before the movies started, and then after they ended, people often went to Henry's Newsstand. Blacks were not allowed to sit at the lunch counter. They were allowed to stand only and to order takeout meals.

The separation of the races was also apparent in living areas. The neighborhoods were definitely segregated. The area in Georgetown where most of the blacks lived was referred to as the "Y" because of the railroad track configuration in that area. Since I did not spend much time in town, the more apparent separation to me was in the rural areas. There were small enclaves where large groups of blacks resided, often former migrant worker camps and other areas where extended families might live.

There were also areas of another group of people who were primarily farmers. They had names like Harmon, Norwood, Davis, Draine, Johnson and others. They did not live in the enclaves with the blacks but often owned their farms and businesses. In many instances, they were as fair-skinned as the whites and did not speak with the black dialect, but they were required to attend the black schools. They predominated in the Long Neck, Angola and Fairmount areas and were commonly referred to as "Moors" or "high yellows." They were, in fact, Nanticokes and other coastal Indians. I highly recommend reading the book "Delaware's Forgotten Folk" by C.A. Weslager for a complete and riveting history of this unique group of people.

There was definitely more awareness of our racial divide during the mid to late 1960's. Most of our awareness come from the national news media and did not have a direct impact on us from the standpoint that we did not have riots and sit-ins locally. H. Rap Brown lived on the Delmarva Peninsula and garnered national attention with his rhetoric in Cambridge, Maryland. Wilmington also became a hotbed of racial strife and actually shaped an election in 1968 for Governor. The local discussions usually revolved around the term "separate but equal," or wondering why the outside agitators were creating problems. Everyone agreed that the "colored" people around here were good people who didn't want to riot or create problems.

Each community had what was known as the "colored" school for elementary students. There was only one "colored" high school in the county being Jason High School. This school is Richard Allen School in Georgetown. Richard Allen was born into slavery in Pennsylvania, and he and his family were sold to a family near Dover, Del. He taught himself to read and write and rose to be a minister, educator, and writer as well as the founder of the African Methodist Episcopal Church. Photo courtesy of Delaware Public Archives.

Rural Life in the 1950's and 60's

> **News in Br'f** *July 20, 1967*
>
> A committee of 15 teenagers met with the Georgetown Jaycees Wednesday evening to discuss the prospect of starting a teenage center. The teenagers have stated that Negroes should be included in the center. So far no Negro youths have expressed interest.
>
> * * * * * *

Although the everyday language referenced "colored people" or "the coloreds", newspapers, textbooks and other formal writings referred to "Negroes".

When our school was integrated, we had some new teachers in addition to the new students. One was Bill Davis, a Nanticoke Indian of Oak Orchard, who was our academic math, trigonometry and calculus teacher. He became our class sponsor and was so loved by our class that we dedicated our yearbook in his honor. One day, he discussed segregation and its impacts with our class. I remember many of us being shocked by what he said. His talk allowed us to view the issue in ways we had never considered before. He is still a friend today.

Bill Davis with Gail Larson, John Thornes, Alta Workman, and Linden Panuska. This picture was part of the Class Dedication to Mr. Davis in the 1968 yearbook. Photo from the Golden Herald.

Chesapeake Bay Bridge

On July 30, 1952, the Cheseapeake Bay Bridge, connecting the Delmarva peninsula to metropolitan areas such as Baltimore and Washington DC, was opened to vehicular traffic.

Accents

The locals in our area do have a unique accent and I have often been told mine is very strong and pronounced. On my first night as a student at the University of Delaware in Newark, I was awakened and asked to come to the lobby. The guys in the dorm had placed bets to guess where I was from. Some had guessed Mississippi, others Virginia, West Virginia, and Alabama; but only one guessed downstate Delaware.

Several years later, while in law school in Williamsburg, Virginia, I was told by a friend from Falls Church, Virginia, that he had finally heard someone with an accent like mine. When I asked who and where, he responded that he saw a commercial for a statewide bank, and there was an Eastern Shore oysterman on the commercial. My friend added, " he sounded just like you."

Our area is on a peninsula—Delmarva—which through my childhood years was very isolated. Until the early 1950's, there was no Bay Bridge over the Chesapeake Bay connecting the peninsula to the Western Shore of Maryland. It was not until the 1960's that we were connected to the south with the Chesapeake Bay Bridge Tunnel. Delaware is separated by a canal north of Middletown that is the traditional demarcation line between "upstate" and "downstate." Historically, there has been a great deal of animosity between upstate and downstate. It is quite puzzling to me that people proudly

The Bay Bridge Tunnell connects the Peninsula with the mainland of Virginia in the Norfolk, Virginia Beach, Newport News areas.

refer to "Lower Slower Delaware." When one does, it is an immediate indication that the person is a newcomer.

We did not travel off the peninsula. The first such trip I remember was when I went with the Cub Scouts when I was eight to see the Baltimore Orioles play.

As previously noted, TV did not play a large role in our lives. What television we watched was local and the same with radio. Therefore, everyone we heard sounded like we did.

We have certain words and phrases that are unique, as outlined later in this book, but our pronunciation of certain words such as "push", "bush", "water", "about" is said to be "Elizabethan." Because of the pervasive influence of national TV, many new comers to the area, and our transient society in general, the younger generation does not have our accent. A few pockets maintain the accent, but these are mainly on the Eastern Shores of Maryland and Virginia. This is especially true of the Chesapeake islands, Smith and Tangier. Even some of the games we played as children, such as "London Bridge is Falling Down," are said to be from the Elizabethan period. Because of our isolation, we retained those traits and customs. Actually. I still hold the opinion that it is everyone else that has the accent, not us.

This is St. Georges Bridge over the C and D Canal. This has been for years the unofficial demarcation between upstate and downstate Delaware. Photo courtesy of Delaware Public Archives.

Rural Life in the 1950's and 60's

Memorable Events

There are many events etched in each of our memories. Some of them are national events that all members of my generation remember. I recall my father listening intently to President Kennedy's speech concerning the Cuban Missile Crisis. I remember my homeroom teacher, Mrs. Jones, announcing to the class that President Kennedy had been shot, and then later that day, telling my father as he worked on the roof of a chicken house. I also remember the assassinations of both Dr. Martin Luther King and Robert F. Kennedy. As important as those events were, for purposes of this chapter, I have focused on the local events that influenced my memory.

HURRICANE HAZEL

Hurricane Hazel first made landfall in North Carolina in 1954 .as a Category four storm. She was responsible for 95 deaths on the United States mainland. The amount of death and total destruction caused the name "Hurricane Hazel" to be retired from usage for any future North American hurricanes. I remember that Jimmie Truitt's shed blew down, as well as a shed at Harold West's. I was only four when Hazel hit, but it did leave some vivid memories. My only recollection of the storm itself was Mom setting the coal-oil lamps (today they are referred to as kerosene) and making sure we had plenty of coal-oil for refills if necessary. After the storm, I noticed many tree limbs broken and laying in the yard. Phone and power lines were down, and many chicken houses and sheds in the neighborhood were destroyed. Jimmie Truitt, Jr. tells of seeing my father and Billy Perry and some other neighbors helping others catch chickens after the chicken houses blew down during the storm.

Chicken houses, sheds, and barns were flattened throughout the County by the high winds. Photo courtesy of Delaware Public Archives.

The combination of rains and high winds caused these power poles to blow over in Georgetown. Photo courtesy of Delaware Public Archives.

MARCH '62 STORM

The most damaging coastal storm in Delaware's history was, surprisingly enough, not a hurricane at all. In 1962, a nor'easter with 70 mile per hour winds pounded the coastal areas for three days over a period of five high tides that were at their monthly peak. The storm caused millions of dollars in damages and killed seven people with more injured. Waves were reported to be in the 20 to 30 foot range, and the storm surge of 9.5 feet was the highest ever reported at the mouth of the Delaware Bay.

I was in Sixth Grade, and the first I knew anything special about the nor'easter was that Mrs. Elliott, a Fifth Grade teacher, was very upset. She had a cottage at the beach which apparently had suffered some damage. The National Guard was called out to evacuate the area and to prevent looting. After the storm,

it was a common activity for people to ride to the beach to see the damage after the National Guard left. I remember hearing about local contractor, Melvin Joseph, a lot at that time. He got bulldozers from all over the country to rebuild the dunes.

HARRINGTON FAIR

As a child I often heard talk of the Harrington Fair (pronounced "Herrinton" by locals). In fact, at that time it was really the Kent and Sussex Fair. The fair did not become the State Fair until January 26, 1962. Even though it was officially changed at that time, it was still referred to as the "Herrinton" fair through the 1960's and into the 1970's. I heard about the fair mainly in regards to the weather. If it was a dry summer, everyone proclaimed that we would get relief and get plenty of rain soon. It was a known "fact" that it always rained during fair week. At that time, the fair consisted of the grandstand and racetrack, the midway, where the rides and carnival activities were located, and the display areas for the many animals that were brought and displayed. The areas were not paved around the midway and display areas.

A view of the concession area of the Fair. Photo postcard from the authors collection.

When it was dry, it was extremely dusty, and when it rained, it was muddy. Many stayed in the stables with their prized animals, while others parked camper trailers on the grounds so they could not only stay with their animals but also enjoy the sights and sounds of the fair.

A view of the of the amusement or "midway" area of the Fair Photo courtesy of Delaware Digital Postcard Collection, University of Delaware Library, Newark, Delaware..

ROCKET SLED

As mentioned elsewhere, the airport was simply an abandoned World War II airfield. A company called All-American Engineering maintained a facility at the airport. They were involved in many projects, one of which was the testing of the strength of certain stopping devises. They launched a rocket sled down the runway toward a stopping devise of webbing and cables. I remember many times being on the school bus while we and all other traffic were flagged down and stopped for the launch. Everyone waited in anticipation and watched as the sled sped down the runway. On more than one occasion, the restraining devices broke, and the sled went across the road into Noah Truitt's field.

Above is the launch of the rocket sled and below is the stopping with cables. Photos courtesy of Hagley Museum and Library.

Another project the company was involved with was snagging someone from the ground with a plane and hook. This was an experiment to try to develop ways to rescue airmen who had to evacuate their planes in times of war. Harry Conaway, a part-time town policeman, volunteered to test this procedure and was snagged to safety by a plane.

GROUND HOG

One year while Jimmie Truitt, Jr. was on the tractor working on the Joe Holson farm near the airport, he saw a strange creature running across the field. He then watched it climb a tree[1]. He contacted his father, who chased it down and threw a heavy coat over it. He took it home and built a cage to restrain it. Everyone in the neighborhood came to see this strange beast, but no one knew what it was. We had a minister at the time, Rev. Schultz, who was from Pennsylvania. He saw the critter and pronounced it to be a groundhog[2]. That was the first one that anyone knew to be around this area.

Since that time, they have proliferated and are now quite a pest to local farmers, eating their crops and digging tunnels, which can cause damage to machinery and injury to the operator.

---
1. Although one does not usually equate groundhogs with climbing they can climb trees and they can swim.
2. Groundhogs are referred to as woodchucks in some areas. Both are the same rodent.

BEAVER DAM

Gussie Wright posed in front of his handiwork. One can see benches and bridges behind him. He charged no fee to those who visited his site. Photo courtesy of Delaware Public Archives.

One treat normally reserved for Sundays was a visit to Beaver Dam. It was located just east of St. George's Chapel on Beaver Dam Branch. There was a large beaver dam and some beaver houses within 50 yards or so of the road. The area was well-known because a local Nanticoke Indian, Gussie Wright, built walkways and bridges to make the area accessible. He also built picnic tables and areas for people to view the dam in comfort. There was no charge for use of the area. The bridges and other structures were not built from traditional sawn lumber and salt or creosote treated materials. Instead, he used materials from the site and used only the minimum amount of sawn boards. This area was popular to visit after church, and school children even took field trips there. Today, the dam still can be seen from the road, but unfortunately all of Gussie Wright's handiwork is gone.

Walk ways and bridges along the creek were all made by Gussie Wright and provided a beautiful view and easy access for all that visited. Photo courtesy of Delaware Public Archives.

RETURN DAY

Return Day is the traditional day that Sussex Countians go to Georgetown, the county seat. This tradition started in 1792. The law that moved the county seat from Lewes to Georgetown required that all the votes in Sussex County be cast in Georgetown. People then returned two days later to hear the results. In 1828, a law was passed that allowed people to vote in their own "hundreds" instead of coming to the county seat.

The parades used to travel east to west down Market street then around the Circle as shown here. Photo courtesy of Delaware Public Archives.

The ballot boxes were then transported to Georgetown and opened the following day. The votes were certified by Thursday and then the results were read publicly to the assembled crowd.

Ellery Parker, basting the ox (actually a steer). Traditional ox roast sandwiches are served throughout the day. Photo from the author's collection.

J. Thomas Sharff wrote in his HISTORY OF DELAWARE in 1888 that Return Day was a festive occasion:

"Booths, stalls and stands are erected near the courthouse, where all kinds of edibles, such as opossum and rabbit meat, fish and oysters, can be procured. The women, who constitute a considerable portion of the crowd, are generously treated to cakes, candies and the best the booths afford."

There is a parade in which the winners and losers for each office ride together, often in horse drawn carriages. The announcement of the returns, a ceremonial burying the hatchet and an ox roast follow. Traditionally, many homes in Georgetown were open for parties and socials.

Listening to the returns in 1962. Note that most men are dressed in suits or sport coats and ties. Photo courtesy of Delaware Public Archives.

Return Day on the Circle in 1894. Photo courtesy of Delaware Public Archives.

Rural Life in the 1950's and 60's

This is the 1960 parade, looking from the north to the south side of East Market Street. The Acme Market is now the location of the Department of Justice, the Braun's store was torn down to become the office of Jim Sabo, Esq. That office is now the Administrative Office of the Courts. Photo courtesy of Delaware Public Archives.

Georgetown native, Jimmie Walls, passing out plates of roast ox in the tradition of Return Day. Town Crier, Ronnie Dodd, is in the background with top hat and glasses Photo courtesy of Delaware Public Archives.

THE INLET BRIDGE COLLAPSE

In this time of controversy over recent failures concerning the construction of a new Indian River Inlet bridge, there have been many references to the collapse of an earlier inlet bridge in 1948.

Prior to 1928, the inlet was a natural inlet from the inland bays to the Atlantic Ocean. That meant there were no artificial jetties in place, and the inlet shifted naturally up and down an approximately two mile stretch of beach.

The snow and ice flows can be seen in this photo taken after the collapse. Photo courtesy of the Delaware Public Archives.

The first bridge was a timber bridge, built in 1934, which was replaced by a concrete and steel, swing-bridge in 1938. This swing bridge was the one that collapsed in 1948, due to scouring from heavy ice flows.

Even though the collapse occurred two years before my birth, it is a vivid memory because Bill Quesada, father of one of my classmates, Steve Quesada, was one of the survivors of the collapse. Three vehicles were on the bridge when it collapsed.

Another view of the bridge after the 1948 collapse. This picture shows the torrid current in the Inlet. Photo courtesy of Delaware Public Archives.

Rural Life in the 1950's and 60's

The lead vehicle was caught in a crack as the bridge started to fail. Mr. Quesada and two others, who were in one of the trailing vehicles, attempted to save the passengers of that vehicle, but the bridge collapsed, plunging all into the frigid waters.

Mr. Quesada later recounted that it took him two days to thaw out from the icy waters of the inlet. Two people, including Mr. Quesada, survived and three perished.

Lore/Tales/Tidbits/Brief Notes

BRAWN

My Uncle Carlton has often recounted the story of three young men in the neighborhood when he was growing up. These men lived past (further from town than) Wilson's Store. The tradition of the time was for people to go to town on Saturday nights and do their "dealin," which meant shopping, bartering, etc.[1] They would also park along the street and socialize. These three young men had a car, but unfortunately, it was not in running condition. In order to maintain a certain status, they pushed their car every Saturday afternoon from their home to Georgetown. Years later it was learned that they had removed the motor from the car to lighten the load.

People came to town on Saturday night to do their "dealin'" and to visit with friends. They sat in their cars and socialized with passerbys. Saturday night was eagerly anticipated by all rural families. Photo courtesy of Delaware Digital Postcard Collection, University of Delaware Library, Newark, Delaware.

---

1. Because stores were open late Saturday, storekeepers traditionally closed on Wednesday afternoon.

THE HUNTER

As a young child, I often heard Uncle Charles and Dad speak with laughter of the Pennsylvania hunter. They were working at Moore Brothers one day when a hunter from Pennsylvania approached and told them he had just shot a pheasant. They were surprised, since we did not have pheasant in the area and they had not seen one except in pictures. They asked to see it and immediately saw that the "pheasant" was one of Joe Holson's bantam roosters.

A Ring Neck Pheasant male has bright plumage with a bright green head. Even a novice hunter should know the difference between the cock bird and a bantam rooster.

A Bantum rooster is much smaller than the traditional roosters of the area and has very bright plumage.

NOON FIRE WHISTLE

Every Saturday at noon the Georgetown fire whistle sounded. We could hear it on the farm if the wind was right. It is a tradition that no longer occurs. I always thought it was a way to let workers know the time, but it was for an entirely different reason. At that time, there were only 50 to 75 fire alarms per year. It was a weekly test to make sure the siren still worked, since there was such a period of time between the siren sounding. Today, there may be 400 alarms per year, so there is no need for the weekly test.

The fire trucks are on display in front of the single bay fire house on the Circle. Photo courtesy of Delaware Public Archives.

BURNT SWAMP

A. Mom was always afraid of forest fires. She remembered the "Burnt," as the Great Cypress Swamp was known, burning for years. It burned the logs and peat under the surface and at times flared up into the open. She said the smell of burning was very strong. She also stated that at times the night sky would be bright in the south from the fire. I did not realize until the last couple of years how this was possible. There have been recent fires in the Carolinas and Virginia, which we have been able to smell here in southern Delaware.

B. Tales of strange creatures in the swamp have circulated for years The stories seemed to always start with young people, and many thought it was merely the imagination or pranks of teens, and it often was. In the mid-1960's, there were tales of a swamp monster, but it turned out to be a practical joke played by a local reporter. However, not many generations ago, bear were trapped in the swamp. The English Botanist Thomas Nuttall ventured deep into the swamp in 1809 to find rare plant species. In a letter dated June 16, 1809, he states "...there are bears not infrequently met with, as many as seven having been caught not many months back."

This raid on a "still" in the Burnt Swamp has caused many to wonder if tales of swamp monsters were simply a way to keep prying eyes out of the swamp. Photo courtesy of Delaware Public Archives.

THE GEORGETOWN DEMONSTRATION SCHOOL

Dad often remarked that when he started attending school in Georgetown, he went to an experimental school. He stated that if he wanted, he could get up and work on a carpentry project either in class or outside, and he could go outside to work in a garden. In 1930, a private group of wealthy individuals, working with the State Board of Education, selected

The author's father is shown seated in the back row in front of the students doing a carpentry project. He is looking at the camera and is seated next to "Fritz" Booth, father of State Senator Joe Booth. Note the knickers pants and the knee high socks. Photo courtesy of the Hagley Museum and Village.

Georgetown as the location for an experiment in progressive education. The teachers selected for this project were sent to a progressive college in the midwest for additional training, and 10 teachers were actually housed in the old Farmer's Bank building on the circle. Instead of the rote learning of the "3 Rs," the students went on field trips and learned by applying their lessons to everyday situations, thus the gardening and building construction. The program only lasted three years because of distrust among the parents. They did not like the noise and disorganized classrooms.

THE LITTLE ENGINE THAT COULD

The author of this famous children's book has a Sussex connection. She was the grandmother of Linford Faucett of Massey's Landing fame. Her name was Francis Ford and the book was originally titled "The Pony Engine." It was written as a Sunday School lesson under the pseudonym, "Uncle Nat." She was born and raised in Philadelphia and traveled by covered wagon to Chicago, where she worked at the "Chicago Tribune." At one point, she worked with Carl Sandburg while in Chicago. Unfortunately, even though her authorship of the book was well documented, she was not recognized or given credit for this work during her lifetime. Her cousin took up her cause in an attempt to get her the credit she deserved for the book. One publisher did give Ms. Ford credit in their version of the book which resulted in litigation between rival publishers. The case was resolved in 1955, which allowed the book to be published under the title "The Pony Engine." Unfortunately, she never received the credit due her until 1957, one year after her death at the age of 102.

FOX HUNTING

There was a group of fox hunters in the neighborhood, most notably Jimmie Truitt, Sr. His son, Jimmie, Jr, still continues the tradition to this day. This was not the talley-ho fox hunting on horses. Instead, it was a group of men who loved to hear their dogs in pursuit of a fox. The fox was not killed, but lived for a chase another day. The men had dog boxes in the backs of their pickups to transport their hounds. They were turned loose in areas that were known to have fox dens. When the dogs got on the trail, the men quickly determined which way the fox was headed and drove their pickups around back-country roads to better hear and possibly catch a glimpse of the dogs and the fox. It amazed me that the men each knew the sound of their own dog and the position of their dog by its baying. I would often hear Jimmie say that he heard Lucy "'tonguing" and that

Lark, a fox hound owned by Jimmie Truitt, is leaving her box ready to trail a fox. The hounds were transported in box, like the one below and to the right, in the back of pickups. Photos by the author.

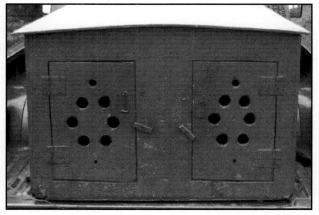

she was in the lead. I can assure you that I could not tell which dog was barking nor which was in the lead.

As a child, my memory was of Jimmie Truitt and Dale Pepper, and in later years, Jimmie Sr. and Jr, Bill Davis of near Oak Orchard, Charlie Koppel and Norman Short of Georgetown being the main participants. Because of the increase in population, this sport is quickly dying out. Once the dogs are turned loose, there is no controlling where they go. People today do not take kindly to seeing a pack of fox hounds running across their yards.

NOXZEMA

There is some mystery and controversy about who actually invented Noxzema. By some accounts it was invented by Dr Francis J Townsend, a doctor/druggest in Ocean City, Md. According to that account, it was originally called "Townsend's R22" and referred to as "no-eczema sunburn ointment". According to that version, he gave it to Dr. George Avery Bunting, a relative who referred to it as "Dr. Bunting's Sunburn Remedy."

By other accounts it was actually invented by Dr. Bunting, of the Ocean View area, supposedly in his coffee pot. There is no doubt however, that Dr. Bunting was responsible for its widespread distribution and the growth of the company. Many Georgetown residents, including the Townsends and Bramhalls, invested in his company and became quite wealthy as a result.

Noxema was known for its cobalt blue bottle and distinctive smell. The creamy salve was cool to the touch. Photo by author courtesy of Charles "Cap" and Jean Wilkins.

According to George Bramhall, a retired attorney from Georgetown and grandson of EbenTownsend, Dr. George A Bunting of Baltimore was the one who invented Noxzema. Dr. Bunting then approached Mr. Eben Townsend, who was wealthy, and asked for his assistance in funding and growing the company. Mr. Townsend's second wife was Nora Bunting, sister of Dr. Bunting, the connection between the two. For his investment Mr. Townsend acquired a substantial amount of stock in the company that later became the Noxell Corporation (in 1990 it was acquired by Proctor and Gamble). George Bramhall, whose mother was a daughter of Mr. Townsend, remembers his mother receiving cases of Noxzema at Christmas. She had plenty for all her friends. One of his mother's brothers, Charles Townsend of Vines Creek, was a mail carrier in the Ocean View area. Local historian, Dick Carter, remembers his grandmother talking about her mailman (Charles Townsend) being a millionaire.

Rural Life in the 1950's and 60's

DUNKARDS

The first time I went to the weekly Dover auction, I saw people who were not dressed like us and were very prevalent at the livestock auctions. Some men had beards, but no mustaches, and they wore hats. Even though they wore blue jeans, theirs were different from everyone else's. When I left, Dad told me they were Dunkards and that they did not drive cars or other motor vehicles. The men that were married had beards. The clothing looked different because there were no buttons, zippers or other adornments. They were referred to as Dunkards because they were totally immersed during baptism. They are still very prevalent west of Dover, Delaware, but are referred to today as the "Amish."

Traditional Amish carriages such as this are still seen on the roads west of Dover. Today they sport the slow moving vehicle triangular sign often seen on farm machinery. They also have side view mirrors and battery powered lights as seen on the carriages in the funeral procession on bottom left. In the photo above, note the vehicles in the parking lot. To the left, Amish women are making doughnuts. Even though modern farm machinery is available, they still use horse-drawn implements. Below, an Amish farmer cuts hay with a horse-drawn sickle. Photos courtesy of Delaware Agricultural Museum and Village.

Sayings, Expressions, Proverbs

1. If a snapping turtle bites you, it will hold on until sundown

2. If you kill a snake, it will wiggle until sundown

3. If you kill a snake and put it on a fence post, it will rain

4. I'm fix'n to do that (meaning I'm getting ready to do that)

5. When your foot itches, it means you will set foot on new ground

6. When your ears burn, someone is talking about you

7. When your nose itches, company is coming

8. When blackbirds swarm the fields in winter, severe weather is coming

9. Black, thick coats on caterpillars means a cold winter

10. A stitch in time saves nine

11. A penny saved is a penny earned

12. Waste Not, Want Not

13. Full as a tick

14. Hard as a brickbat

15. How about that

16. Heavens to Betsy

17. For the love of Pete

18. Hope to die

19. As sure as shooting

20. No siree Bob

21. God willing and if the creek don't rise

22. She was dressed to the nines

23. Can't hold a candle to...(isn't as good as)

24. Quick as a flash

25. Faster than greased lightning

26. When one had a birthday and for example it was the 60th, the old timers referred to it as being in their 61st.

27. It (often pronounced "hit") favors rain

28. Dog tired

29. I'm plumb tuckered out

30. My get up and go has got up and gone

31. He got his come - uppance...cut down to size...showed up

32. Too big for/her britches

33. A clodhopper (a clumsy person)

33. He's no great shakes

34. He talks out of both sides of his mouth

35. Doesn't have all his marbles

36. Happy as a June Bug

37. Go every whichways

38. "Down below" when referring to - Millsboro, Dagsboro, Gumboro or any towns

south of Georgetown

39. Cut half in two (cut in half)

40. Do ones dealing (shopping)

41. Smack dab (exactly)

42. Whereabouts

43. No account (good for nothing)

44. To act up (misbehave)

45. Shat (pine needle)

46. Trying to catch a cold

47. Have no truck with (ignore)

48. Looking for a needle in a haystack

49. A watched pot never boils

50. Too many cooks spoil the broth

51. Birds of a feather flock together

52. A new broom sweeps clean

53. God helps those that help themselves

54. Beware of a wolf in sheep's clothing

55. Idle hands are the devils workshop

56. All work and no play makes for a dull boy

57. Beauty is only skin deep

58. You can catch more flies with sugar (or honey) than vinegar

59. Out of round

60. "St.Swithen's Day if it does rain, for forty days it will remain; St. Swithen's Day if it be fair, for 40 days it will rain no more." St. Swithen's Day is July 15. Basil Perry is the only person, except my father when he was quoting Basil

Rural Life in the 1950's and 60's

Perry, that I ever heard mention this.

61. You look like the last rose of summer (this meant one looked tired and wilted)

62. Enough to gag a maggott (something very sickening)

63. Jump from the frying pan into the fire (go from a bad to situation to one worse)

64. Now we're cooking with gas (making progress)

65. Three sheets to the wind (intoxicated)

66. Drunk as a hoot owl (intoxicated)

67. Fallin' down drunk (intoxicated)

68. Don't have to have a tree fall on my head to know it hurts

69. That dog don't hunt (I don't beleive what you said. It doesn't make sense)

70. Elbow grease

71. Pipjenny (a small bump or pimple, this term is almost exclusively used on the Delmarva Peninsula

72. Shine

73. I don't have a dog in that fight (meaning I have no reason to get involved in this argument)

74. Holy Smokes!

75. Holy Mackeral!

Appendices

Appendix I
Family Tree

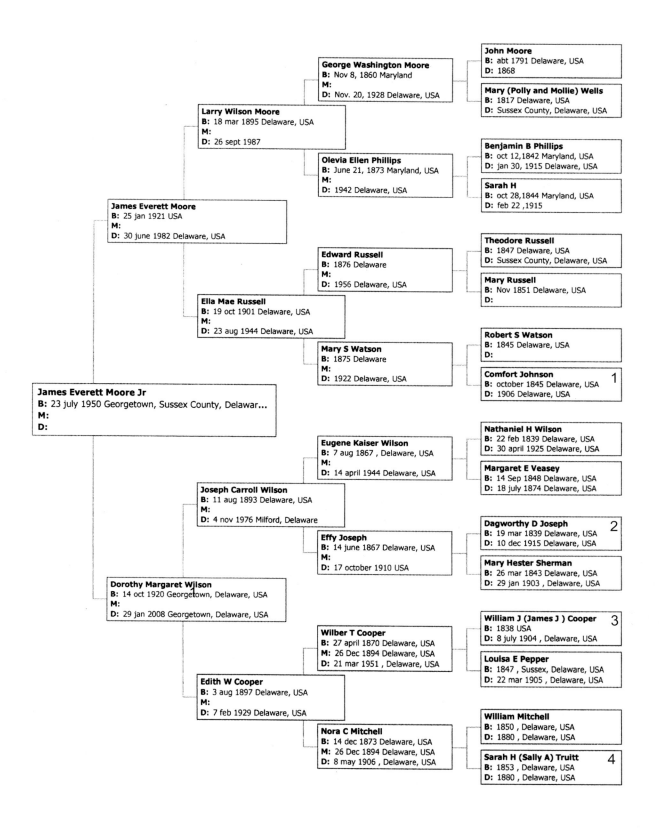

1. Johnson continued on page 198
2. Joseph continued on page 199
3. Cooper continued on page 200
4. Truitt continued on page 201

Growin' Up Country

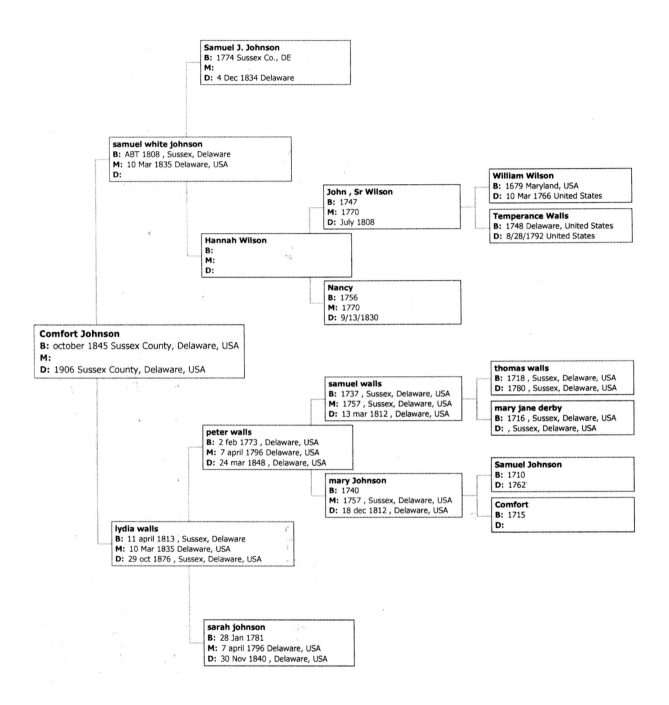

Continued from number 1 "Johnson" from page 197

Rural Life in the 1950's and 60's

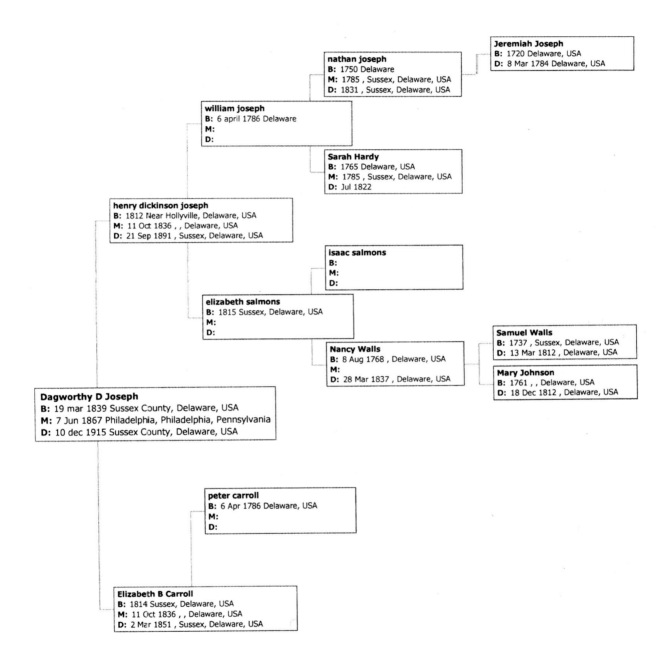

Continued from number 2 "Joseph" from page 197

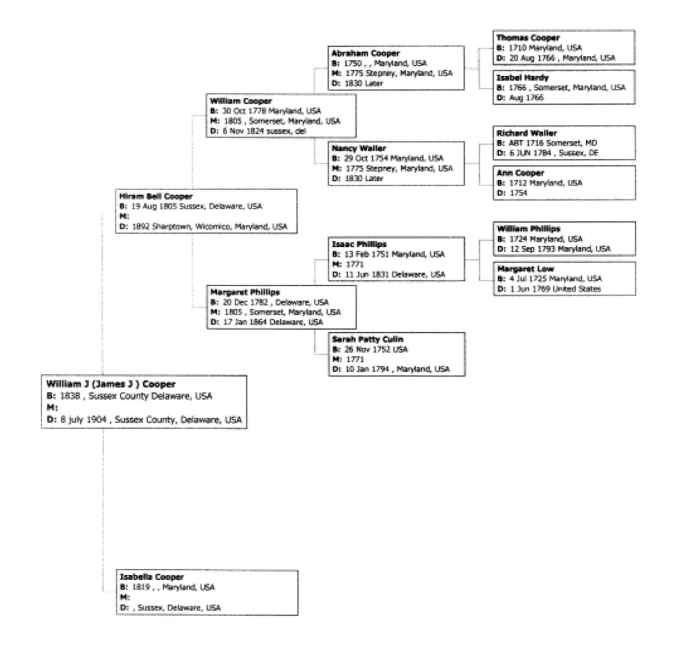

Continued from number 3 "Cooper" from page 197

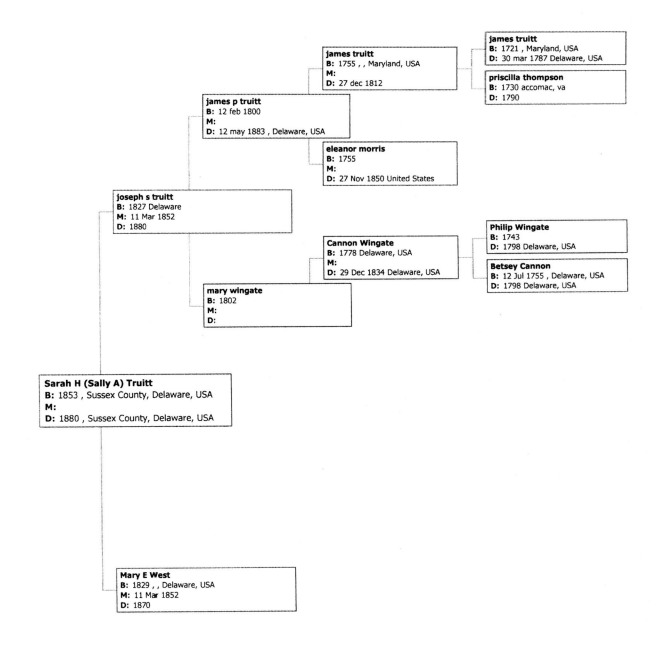

Continued from number 4 "Truitt" from page 197

Appendix II
Pop Pop's Poetry

Rural Life in the 1950's and 60's

Ella

I knew a lady in years gone by,
And a lady is what I mean.
She lived a very wholesome life,
And kept her records clean.

When Sunday came around,
She always kept it holy.
The other days she served her Christ,
The one that is meek and lowly.

She talked about her neighbors some,
When she was in the mood.
But she never talked about the bad,
She talked about the good.

She never talked harsh to anyone.
She had a heart that was not stony.
The life she lived seven days a week
Was her living testimony.

She loved her children and her home,
And loved her neighbors, too.
But God saw fit to take her home
Away beyond the blue.

If you wonder why I knew so much
About this lady's life,
And have not guessed, I'll tell you now:
T'was because she was my wife.

I expect to meet her some glad day
And say, "Ella, dear, good morning.
There's been many dark nights since you went away
But now a new day is dawning."

A Christmas Present For The Needy

God gave a Christmas present
To a world that was in need.
They were disobedient to his command,
A repetition of Adam's seed.

Yes, a present was given
About two thousand years ago,
By the Father of all mankind
Because he loved them so.

The present was the baby Jesus,
Born in a Judean town,
To the humble Virgin Mary,
Previously without fame or renown.

Yes, God gave to a needy people
And we should do the same,
Not to get something in return
And not to get glory and fame.

The wise men gave gifts to Jesus
On the very first Christmas day,
While lying in the stable
Tucked in a bed of hay.

When Jesus grew up to be a man,
He went about doing good,
Healing broken bodies,
Helping everyone he could.

And if he were here in person,
We could hear him say take heed.
Don't give for a gift in return,
But give to those in need.

Obey God, And Love Your Fellow Man

God told Adam and Eve in the garden of Eden,
To not eat from a certain tree,
And what he said to Adam and Eve,
He says to you and me.

Now, if we read God's Holy Word,
From Genesis to Revelation,
Then try to abide by what he says,
T'will be a great consolation.

But if we do as Adam and Eve,
And take our advice from the serpent,
We're only condemning ourselves to die,
And that is sure and certain.

Now, Adam and Eve, they had two sons,
Their names were Able and Cain,
They went out into the field one day,
But only one there did remain.

For jealousy got into the heart of Cain,
And then he slew his brother,
And from that day on even till now,
We've been trying to devour each other.

Please God, forbid that we should walk,
In the footsteps of our brother, Cain,
For if we do, Christ's death on the cross,
For us it will be in vain.

Christ told his disciples a long time ago,
There's one thing I command you to do,
That is to love one another,
As I also have loved you.

If we love our neighbor as ourself,
And God with all our heart, soul and mind,
We could go out and meet our neighbors abroad,
And leave our guns behind.

We spend billions of dollars every year,
For guns and ammunition,
But someday man will touch off a bomb,
And blow us all into oblivion.

If man would leave these bombs alone,
And would turn to the mighty sword,
We could lick the world with kindness,
And win them for the Lord.

Of course, the sword I'm speaking of,
Is the mighty word of God,
So let's spend our billions every year,
To spread God's Holy Word.

But if we talk about the billions,
We'll howl about the cost,
But Christ came not to destroy the world,
He came to seek and save the lost.

Then if I kill my enemy here,
No one can ever tell,
Instead of winning his soul for Christ,
I might send both his soul and mine to Hell.

Appendix III
History of St. John's Church

St. John's: A History

By: Mr. and Mrs. Everett Moore
Edited by: J. Everett Moore Jr.

St. John's was first organized as "Johnson's Society," in the 1830's. The meetings were held in private homes and later in the Springfield Free School, District 33, building, which now serves as Wilson's store.

On the 21st of May, 1852, the Society met in the school to consider the possibility of building a church at or near Springfield Crossroads. After prayer by their pastor, John Hough, and some discussion, it was resolved to build a church as soon as possible and the sum of $210.00 was subscribed before parting. After this resolution was made known to the Quarterly Conference in Georgetown on June 20, 1852, a building committee of seven persons was appointed, with John Hough serving as the chairman.

Approximately one acre of land was purchased from a tract of land known as "Springfield" on July 27, 1852. The frame of the Church was raised on Saturday, September 11, 1852. On March 7, 1854, all debts, except $18.50 were paid off.

The first record of a burial was in May, 1853, although there is evidence that there may have been earlier burials. A meeting was held on Wednesday, November 12, 1857, to lay off the burial ground in lots and to choose a way to raise money to erect a fence. It was decided that anyone who wanted a cemetery lot would pay a "certain sum" which would be used in the erection of the fence.

An additional 7,000 square feet of land was acquired on December 19, 1874, for the cemetery. This land was laid out in lots of 60 by 9 feet.

On September 21, 1892, it was agreed that the original Church be enlarged by adding an eight-foot recessed pulpit.

The trustees met on March 8, 1892, for the purpose of forming a circuit.[1] An agreement was made with the Conference for the following Churches to form this Circuit: St. John's, Sandhill, Cokesbury, and Bethesda. St. John's continues to be part of the Georgetown Circuit with Bethesda and Providence Churches.[2]

As early as 1904, meetings were being held to consider whether to build a new church or repair the old one. In 1907 a new church was erected. This is the same church that is in use today.

The contract price on the present church was $2,148.20. The art glass windows, pews, pulpits and other furnishings were contracted for as extras, bringing the total cost to $3,515.38.

Services in the old Church were discontinued and the building was sold on October 3, 1908, for $78.25 to William Wilson, who moved it to his farm in front of the Church. It was used as a barn until it was torn down in 1956.

---

1. A Circuit is two or more Churches served by one minister.
2. The original Circuit of St. John's, Bethesda, Cokesbury, and Sandhill remained together from 1892 until 1955. In 1955, the Circuit was changed to St. John's, Bethesda, Providence, and Zoar Churches. In 1975, Zoar left the Circuit, leaving the remaining three as the Circuit which remains today.

The community hall was moved from the CCC Camp near Georgetown in 1950, for use as a Sunday School and social hall. It was totally renovated in 1955. Bathrooms were added at that time. Prior to that time, outside toilets were used.

The church was placed on the National Register of Historic Places on July 12, 1990. There is a Delaware Historic Marker on the site with a brief history of the Church.

First Trustees

Henry O. Bennum - (Chairman)

James P. Walls - (Secretary)

Peter Rust

John M. Hopkins

William M. Johnson

Silas Smith

Nathaniel M. Johnson

Treasurers of St. John's Cemetery

Albert J. Johnson - appointed December 28, 1874
1874-1898 (24 years)

T.A. West - elected May 10, 1898
1898-1924 (26 years)

George A. Wilson - Elected March 20, 1924
1924-1932 (8 years)

Larry W. Moore, Treasurer - 1932-1971 (39 years)

J. Everett Moore Sr., Treasurer
1971 until his death on June 30, 1982

Mrs. J. Everett Moore Sr., assisted by son, Merrill C. Moore
June 30, 1982 until her death on Jan. 29, 2007

Merrill C. Moore Jan. 29, 2007- present

Rural Life in the 1950's and 60's

Ministers of St. John's Church, 1892-2010

Andrew D. Davis	March 22, 1892	March 25, 1895
William R. McFarlane	March 25, 1895	March 24, 1896
Julius A. Brewington	March 24, 1896	March 23, 1897
James T. VanBurkslow	March 23, 1897	March 20, 1899
James H. Wilson	March 20, 1899	March 19, 1902
W.S.H. Williams	March 25, 1902	March, 1904
Harry Taylor	March, 1904	March, 1906
George S. Thomas	March, 1906	March 1911
L. B. Morgan	March, 1911	April 6, 1914
Wm. P. Taylor	April 6, 1914	April, 1916
N. Claude Benson	April, 1916	April, 1919
E. H. Marshall	April, 1919	April, 1921
C. W. Spry	April, 1921	April, 1923
W. J. Donahue	April 6, 1923	April 8, 1926
Walter G. Barlow	April 4, 1926	April, 1928
J. W. Sutton	April, 1928	1929
D. E. Carr	March, 1929	March, 1930
H. M. Ralph	March, 1930	April, 1934
J. H. Gardner	April, 1934	April, 1937
E. N. Wright	April, 1937	May, 1943
W. L. McClintock	May, 1943	1946
M. T. Romans	May, 1946	1947
Edwin C. Thomas	May, 1947	1949
Ira E. Crum	May, 1949	1952
Joseph V. Holliday	May, 1952	1956
Frank Lucia	1956	1959
J. Melvin Shultz	1959	1962
Jeffrey Westfall	1962	1964
Joseph N. Geiger	1964	1966
Edward Peurifoy	1966	1969
Jack Rozelle	1969	1970
Edward C. Goodley	1970	1973
Hubert F. Jicha, Jr.	1973	1975
Austin L. Brittingham	1975	1980
William S. Downing	1980	November, 1981
Theodore Swager	January, 1982	June 12, 1983
Paul E. McCoy	June 19, 1983	July 10, 1983
James B. Doughten	July 24, 1983	June 3, 1984

Sam McWilliams	June 10, 1984	June 26, 1988
Donald Clendaniel II	July 3, 1988	June 30, 1991
Debra Lindsay-Hudgins	July 7, 1991	June 30, 1998
Paige Marshall	July 5, 1998	June 10, 2001
Robert D. Howell	July 1, 2001	May 25, 2003
Ron Schatz	June 1, 2003	June 30, 2008
Carol E. Svecz	July 1, 2008	Present

Compiled by Mr. and Mrs. J. Everett Moore and Teresa Moore Adams

Rev. William P. Taylor served St. Johns from April 16, 1914 to April 1916. Photo from the collection of Mr. and Mrs. J Everett Moore, Sr

Rev. George Sanford Thomas served St. Johns from 1906 to 1911. Please note the Circuit included St. Johns, Bethesda, Cokesbury and Sandhill. Photo from the collection of Mr. and Mrs. J. Everett Moore, Sr.

Rural Life in the 1950's and 60's

Real Estate Acquisitions

July 27, 1852
  The first tract of land, known as Springfield was from James E. Blizzard and wife Mary Ann to Henry O. Bennum, Peter Rust, James P. Walls, John M. Hopkins, William M. Johson, Silas Smith, Nathaniel M. Johnson, Trustees, one acre approximately - sum of $75.00.

December 19, 1874
  From Peter Rust and wife Harriet to Henry O. Bennum, Peter P. Dodd, William Hancock and Peter Rust of Georgetown Hundred and Albert J. Johnson, Josiah Simpler, John C. Walls, John Walls and Paynter Frame of Indian River, 7,000 square feet. (For burial ground - May be sold of in Lots of the size of 60 feet by 9 feet).

August 13, 1894
  From Charles H. Joseph and wife Sarah E. to Trustees, Peter P. Dodd, Gilly Walls, Kendall D. Wilson, Josiah G. Simpler, Nathaniel H. Wilson, Paynter Frame, Albert J. Johnson, Peter W. Rust, John H. Dodd, 1/8 acre more or less.

May 29, 1956
  From Lula May Hitchens to Trustees St. John's M.E. Church, approximately 1/4 acre (for Grove Corner)

May 31, 1971
  From Bonard Brittingham and Helen Brittingham his wife to Trustees of St. John's M.E. Church, 1.4569 acres, for addition to cemetery.

Rev. Ira Crumb served St. John's from 1949 to 1952. Photo from the collection of Mr. and Mrs. J. Everett Moore, Sr.

A meeting was held at Springfield School house (the usual place of worship for "Johnsons Society") on 27th May. 1852 to take into consideration the propriety of Building a church at or near Springfield cross roads. Revd John Hough present, after prayer by our minister and some consultation. It was agreed to build one as soon as practicable. A Subscription was straightway got up and the sum of two hundred and ten dollars was subscribed before parting. —

The above resolution was made known to the Quarterly meeting conference held at Geo:town on 20th June following, whereupon the following building committee was appointed. to wit. Peter Rust, John Hopkins, Silas M. Warington, Henry O. Bennum, Revd John Hough (the preacher in charge,) James P. Walls and John Walls — at which time it was agreed to give legal notice to the members of Johnsons Society that a meeting of Sd. Society will be held on 3rd of July 1852 for the purpose of electing trustees for Sd. Society at 5 o'clock P.M. of Sd. day which was done, and the meeting accordingly held, a copy of which follows

At a meeting of the members of the Methodist Episcopal church Belonging to Johnsons Society, (near Springfield cross roads) on Saturday the 3rd day of July at 5h o'clock P.M. 1852, for the purpose of Electing a board of trustees for said Society, in accordance with notice previously given. Henry O. Bennum was called to the chair, and James P. Walls, appointed Secretary, whereupon the following persons were elected as trustees for Said Society, towit: Henry. O. Bennum, Peter Rust, James P. Walls, John M. Hopkins, William M. Johnson, Silas Smith and Nathaniel M. Johnson. On motion the meeting adjourned —

Henry O. Bennum chairn

Attest James P. Walls, Secy

The frame of the church was raised on Saturday 11th day of September 1852, at which time the trustees agreed to make Henry O. Bennum the chairman of the board of Trustees, and James P. Walls the Secretary.

Above is the copy of the original minutes of Johnson's Society authorizing the formation of St. John's Church. The meeting was held in Springfield Free School #33 (the building that now houses Wilson's Store). See the next page for a typed transcript.

Rural Life in the 1950's and 60's

A meeting was held at Springfield School house (the usual place of worship for "Johnson's Society") on 27th May, 1852 to take into consideration the propriety of Building a church at or near Springfield cross roads. Rev. John Hough present after prayer by our minister and some consultation, It was agreed. to build one as soon as practicable. A subscription was straightway got up and the sum of two hundred and ten dollars was subscribed before parting.

The above resolution was made known to the Quarterly meeting conference held at Georgetown on 20th June following where upon the following building committee was appointed, to wit, Peter Rust, John Hopkins, Silas M Warrington, Henry O Bennum, Rev. John Houghton(the preacher in charge) James P. Walls and John Walls, at which time it was agreed to give legal notice to the members of Johnson Society that a meeting of Said Society will be held on 3rd of July 1852 for the purpose of electing trustees for Said Society at 5 1/2 o'clock P.M. of said day which was done, and the meeting accordingly held, a copy of which follows

At a meeting of the members of the Methodist Episcopal church Belonging to Johnsons Society, (near Springfield Crossroads) on Saturday the 3rd day of July at 5 1/2 oclock P.M. 1852, for the purpose of Electing, a board of trustees for said Society, in accordance with notice previously given, Henry O Bennum was called to the chair, and James P. Walls, appointed Secretary, whereupon the following persons were elected as trustees for Said Society, to wit, Henry O. Bennum, Peter Rust, James P. Walls, John M. Hopkins, William M. Johnson, Silas Smith and Nathaniel M. Johnson. On motion the meeting adjourned-

Henry O. Bennum, chairman

Attest James B. Walls, Sec

The frame of the church was raised on Saurday 11th day of September 1852, at which time the trustees agreed to make Henry O. Bennum the chairman of the board of Trustees, and James P. Walls the Secretary.

Appendix IV
Mom's Recipes

Pan Spaghetti

1/2 to 1 lb. ground beef
1 (16 oz.) bag egg noodles
4 qt. water
2 (8oz.) cans tomato sauce
salt
pepper

    Brown ground beef. While ground beef is cooking, cook noodles in water according to package directions. Drain ground beef. Drain noodles. Combine ground beef and noodles in tomato sauce in skillet. Add salt and pepper to taste. Simmer, covered, 16 minutes.

Potatoes in Bacon Water

5 medium large white potatoes
4 strips bacon
1-1/2 tsp. salt
pepper

    Fry bacon; drain and put aside, keep grease. Peel and slice potatoes. Add enough water with the grease to cover potatoes; salt and pepper. Cook until tender (boil about 12 to 15 minutes). Break bacon into pieces and add to potatoes.

Biscuits (Old Fashioned)

4 c. flour
4 tsp. baking powder
1-1/3 tsp. salt
5 heaping tsp. Crisco
hot water

    Preheat oven to 400 degrees. Mix flour, salt and baking powder together. Add Crisco and mix all together. Use enough hot water to make a soft dough. Knead well, then make into biscuits. Bake at 400 degrees for about 25-30 minutes. Makes about 21 medium size biscuits.

Yellow Layer Cake

Cake
1 box yellow cake mix
1 pkg. vanilla instant pudding
3 medium size eggs
1-1/2 cups water
1/3 cup vegetable oil

Frosting
3/4 lb. 10x sugar
4 Tbsp. cocoa
1 tsp. vanilla
1 Tbsp. vegetable shortening
Approximately 3-1/2 Tbsp. milk

Preheat oven to 350 degrees. Grease and flour three 9-inch round cake pans. Mix all ingredients for cake together and beat with mixer for 2 minutes. Cool and then frost.

For frosting:
Combine all ingredients, (except milk) and beat with mixer. Add milk gradually to get the right consistency to spread.

Peanut Butter Candy

1 lb. 10x sugar
1 tsp. vanilla
1/3 cup mashed potatoes
    (approximately)
peanut butter (approx. 1/3 to 1/2 lb.)
sprinkle of salt

Mix sugar (put aside 1/2 cup for later), salt, vanilla and enough potatoes to make a soft dough. Sprinkle waxed paper or dumpling board with remaining sugar. Also sprinkle rolling pin and then roll out dough. Spread with peanut butter and roll up like a jelly roll. Slice into small pieces as desired.

Rural Life in the 1950's and 60's

Dumplin's

3 Cups All Purpose Flour
6 Tablespoons Shortening
4 Quarts Rich (Yellow) Chicken Broth*

Salt
1 Cup Warm Water

Place flour and salt in large mixing bowl. Then add shortening and knead until ingredients are mixed. Then add warm water a little at a time while kneading.

Break off small bits of dough and roll to the thickness desired.

After rolling to desired thickness, cut in rectangles approximately 2 inches wide and 4 inches long. They should be put on a floured plate and then floured between layers to prevent them from sticking together.

The broths should be brought to a full boil and then the dumplings should be added one at a time stirring occasionally. They should cook for 15-20 minutes stirring occasionally and keeping a slow boil.

* Can be made with beef, turkey or chicken.

Asparagus Soup

Water
Asparagus
Side Meat (fat meat)
Potatoes
Drop Dumplings
Salt and Pepper

Cut asparagus in 2 inch lengths, put in a pot of water with side meat (best to score the side meat with a sharp knife to the rind). cut potatoes into 1 inch pieces and add to the pot.
Make dough and form into small 1 inch balls. Add them to the pot. Salt and pepper to taste. Bring the mixture to a boil and then simmer until all ingredients are tender. The longer it cooks the better it tastes.

Index

Symbols

3 Bears Nursery 31
5/8 basket 121
20th Century 101
1868 Beers Atlas 109

A

Abbott family 160
Academic 102, 103, 167
accent 169
Acme Market 181
Addison 9
Administrative Office of the Courts 181
Agricultural Museum and Village 7, 57, 79, 89
airmail 155
airport 10, 40, 41, 176, 177
Alabama 169
All American Engineering 40, 176
Allens 50
American Field Service 105
American Motor Company 159
Amish 191
Amos and Andy 143
AM station 140
Anderson Corner Road 159
Angola 166
Apollo 11 162
arithmatic 101
Asbury, John 19
asparagus soup 126, 127
Asparagus Soup 217
Assateague, Indian River 16
As The Land Of Pleasant Living 150
Athletic Council 105
Atlantic Ocean 15, 182
Atrazine 64
auditorium 105
Aunt Hilda 118
Auto Body and Fender 103
automatic feeders 61
automatic milkers 94
Auto Mechanics 103
Avalon Road 100
Ayers' Theater 43

B

Baccularuate 105
bacon 54, 125
  bacon grease 125
Baltimore 17, 19, 31, 99, 150, 168, 170
Band 25, 105, 141
Band Council 105
Bantum rooster 185
Barbering 103
Barlow, Walter G. 209
Barrett's Chapel 19
baseball 37, 38, 39, 104, 109, 110
basketball 39, 104, 105
Bastianelli, Herman 104
bear 186
Beatles 43
Beauty Culture 103
Beaver Dam 178
Beaver Dam Branch 178
Beaver Dam Road 100
Beebe Hospital 132, 134
Bell, Rick 101
Bennum, Henry O. 208, 211
Bennum's Switch 19
Benson, N. Claude 209
Bethel 17
Bethesda 70, 207
Betts, Howard 65
Bible School 27, 70, 72
biddies 59, 60
Biscuits 215
blackbirds 192
black rotary dial phones 137
black snakes 79
black tape 38
Blessing 125
Blizzard, John 57
Blizzard, Mary Ann 211
Blue Hen chickens 17
Blue Hen Rooster 17
Blue Hen Theater 44
Bluerocks Little League Team 36
bobwhite quail 95
Bob Willey & Sons in Milton 141
boiled pig's feet 127
bomb shelters 102
Bonanza 149
Bond Bread 32, 33

Rural Life in the 1950's and 60's

Border State 18
Bowden, Jim 7, 138
box lids 60
Bramhalls 190
Braun's store 181
Breasure, Leroy 69
Brewington, Julius A. 209
Brick Bat 192
Brick Hotel 23, 146
Bridgeville 99
Brinkley, David 150
Brittingham, Austin L. 209
Brittingham, Bonard 211
Broadkill River 17, 159
broiler industry 20
Brown, H. Rap 166
Brttingham, Helen 211
Brynlee 9
buckshot 41
Buick Dealership 160
Building Construction 103, 187
bulldozers 56, 174
bullet rifles 41
Bunting's Sunburn Remedy 190
burial 207
"Burnt" 186
Burton's Chevrolet 160
burying the hatchet 179
Butler, Dr. John 8
butter beans 120, 122, 126

C

cabbage 120, 121, 127
calculators 103
Calverts 16
camp meetings 19
Camporchiaro, Dr. 8
Candy Stripers 105
can opener 124
cantaloupe 122
Cape Henlopen 20
Cape Henlopen School District 99
Carey's Camp 19
Carlton's Men's Store 44
Carr, D.E. 209
carrot 122, 127
Carter, Dick 7
Case 400 tricycle-front tractor 96
Case 800 52, 62
cast iron skillet 125, 127
Castoria 131
Castor Oil 131
catalpa tree 37
Category 4 storm 173
caterpillar 192
Catholic Parish 20

CBS 151
CCC Camp 208
cedar pull handle 82
cheerleading 104
Cheseapeake Bay Bridge 168
"Chicago Tribune" 188
chicken and dumplings 81, 127
chicken catchers 58, 62
chicken coops 57
chicken feet gravy 80
chicken hook 89
Chicken-House Apartments 62
chicken killings 79
chicken neckers 80
chicks 20, 49, 50, 60, 62, 116
chiggers 40
"china" eggs 79
Choptank Indians 16
chores 39, 52, 53, 55, 60, 77, 79, 81, 94, 117
Chorus 105
Christened 70
Christmas 71, 115, 116, 117, 204
  Christmas tree 116
Church 4, 6, 10, 11, 19, 27, 31, 33, 38, 57, 58, 68,
    69, 70, 71, 74, 75, 87, 100, 115, 116, 159, 165,
    166, 169, 178, 206, 207, 208, 209, 211, 213
Circle 18, 21, 22, 24, 25, 118, 134, 146, 156, 160,
    179, 180, 185, 187
Circuit 207
Civil Defense 20, 102
Civilian Conservation Corps 70
Civil War 19, 23
clapboard 81, 86
Clark, Dick 43
Clayton, John M. 99
Clayton Theater 44
Clendaniel, Donald II 210
climbing belt 138
climbing spikes 138
clothes line 28, 53, 54, 82
Clover Farm store 31, 32
coal-oil lamps 173
coal shuttles 59
coal stoves 59
Cober, Helen 101
Cokesbury 207
Coke, Thomas 19
colored people 165, 167
comey-comey 30
Commercial Foods 103
commode 85
Communion 70
Community Hall 70, 71, 115, 208
computers 37, 102, 103, 161
Conaway, Harry 176
Conaway Motors 160, 162

Concord/Seaford 16
Confederate Sympathizers 18
congregational singing 70
corn 55, 92, 120, 122, 126
  corn stalks 55
cornbread 126
corncobs 54
corn "cribs" 64
corn peg 89
corn sheller 64, 79
corn shocks 89
Corvair 159, 161
Counties 15, 16
County Seat 18, 20, 179
Cousin Brucie 142
covered dish dinners 70, 71
cow 29, 55, 94
crocks 59, 60, 66
Cronkite, Walter 151
crowsfoot 116
Crum, Ira E. 209
Cuban missle crisis 102
Cuban Missle Crisis 172
cucumber 122, 125
cucumbers in vinegar 126
cultivators 63
cursive
  writing 101
cut-over 57
cypress shingles 86

D

Dagsboro 16, 17, 44, 159, 193
dairy barn 92
Davis 166
Davis, Andrew D. 209
Davis, Bill 167, 189
"dealin" 184
Deep Branch Road 26, 28, 29, 78, 159
deer 42, 95
Delaware Bay 15, 20, 174
Delaware Camping Center, Inc. 160
Delaware history 62, 101, 146
Delaware Indians 16
"Delaware's Forgotten Folk" 166
Delaware State Archives 7, 15, 16, 18, 31, 58, 60,
    75, 106, 107, 118, 134, 136, 140, 146, 162,
    166, 170, 173, 178, 179, 180, 181, 182
Delaware State Fair 7
Delaware State News 145
Delaware Technical & Community College, Owen's
    Campus 164
Delco 83
Delmarva Peninsula 49, 62, 168, 195
Depression 20, 70, 143
DeSoto 159

detention 102
Dickerson, Edmon 90
Dimondi, Bill 7
Ding Dong School 149
dinner 126
disk 63, 96
Distributive Education 103
Dixon, Jeremiah 16
Doc Smoot 132
Doc Waples 132
Dodd, Peter P. 211
Dodd, Ronnie 7, 181
Doddtown Road 159
Dolly's popcorn 42
Donahue, W.J. 209
Dorey, Louise 73
double sided sickle 56
Doughten, James B. 209
Down below 193
Downing, William S. 209
"downstate" 169
downstate Delaware. 169
Drafting 103
Draine 166
Draper, Tom 7
Dr. Cannon 133
Dr Francis J Townsend 190
Dr. George Bunting 190
Dr. Martin Luther King 172
droughts 64, 110
Dr. Reese Swain 133
Dr. Van 132
Dr. Wildberger 132, 134, 165
DTCC 106
ducks 93
Dulles 162
DuMont 151
Dumplin's 217
Dunkards 191
DuPont Company's Nylon Plant 106
Dutch 15
Dwyer, Don 7

E

Easter 71, 115, 116, 117, 118
  Easter Parade and Promenade 117
Eastern shore of Maryland 15, 49
Eastern Shore oysterman 169
Eckstorm, Elaine 107
Edinger, Warren 133
Ed Sullivan Show 43, 149
egg basket 89
egg beater 124, 125
eggs 29, 47, 79, 85, 125
Electronics 103, 149
"Elizabethan" 170

Rural Life in the 1950's and 60's

Ella 203
Encyclopedia Brittannica 103
English 15, 16, 186
English Bike 38
English Botanist Thomas Nuttall 186
ESSO 160
European settlers 16
Evangel Hour with Rev. Ray Chamberland 151
Evening Journal 83, 146
Exchange Student 43, 105
EXXON 160

F

Fairmount 100, 101, 166
fan belts 161
Farmall A tractor 56
Farmall Cub tractor 121
Farmall H 52, 62, 66
Farmers Bank 22
Farm Mechanics 103
fat meat 126
Faucett, Linford 188
fax machines 49, 103
federal surplus food program 102
Fed Ex 155
feed bag 84
feed bins 61, 92
feed cart 61, 92
feed houses 49, 50
Fenwick 19
Fenwick Island 16
fertilizer 122
field hockey 104
Fighting Blue Hens 17
Fire Prevention Week 107
fish 126, 179
  fish salesman 33
flour sifter 124, 125, 127
Flower Power 43
foddler knife 56
football 38, 39, 59, 100, 104, 109, 117, 132
Ford, Francis 188
Fort Miles 20
four-bottom plow 62
four-row corn planter 63
fox 189
Fox Hunting 189
Frame, Paynter 211
French Club 105
fried chicken 117, 126
fried fish 126
fried pork chops 126
fried steak 126
frog legs 127
funnel corn wagon 65
Future Farmers of America 105

Future Teachers of America 105

G

Garden 29, 56, 83, 88, 92, 95, 96, 120, 121, 122, 187, 205
Gardner, J.H. 209
gas brooder stove 59
Geiger, Joseph N. 209
General John Dagsworthy 16
Georgetown Circuit 70, 207
Georgetown, Delaware 11, 46, 142, 164
Georgetown Demonstration School 187
Georgetown Elementary School 99
Georgetown High School 99, 165
Georgetown Marble and Granite Works 47
Georgetown Post Office 156
Georgetown Raceway 103
Georgetown Socials 145
George Washington 115
Gibson, Jose 106
gizzard 80
Gleason, Jackie 149
Golden Knight 99
Good Friday 115
Goodley, Edward C. 209
Grace 125
Graduation 106
Grant's Store 116
grape arbor 81
grape jelly 81
grater 124
Gravel Hill Road 68, 69
gravity corn-wagon 64
Great Cypress Swamp 186
Greenberger, John B. 150
greens 122, 126
Greenwood 16, 99
Grottos 128
Ground Hog 177
guineas 93
Gumboro 17, 61, 193
Gunsmoke 149

H

Hagley Museum and Library 7, 40, 176, 187
hamburger 126
Hancock, William 211
hand-loomed carpet 78
hand sickle 56
hanging feeder 61
Harmon 166
Harrington Fair 175
Harvard Business Services, Inc. 101
Hazzard, Barbara 107
Health Room 102

heart-healthy 125
heart-pine floors 78
Henlopen Lighthouse 18
Henry's Newstand 43, 160
Hewitt, Frank 7
Highlights for Kids 101
Highway Commission 159
high yellows 166
HISTORY OF DELAWARE 179
Hitchens, Lula May 211
hitching post 84, 85
Hoebee, John 7, 142
hog killing pots 54
Hog killings 54
Holliday, Joseph V. 209
Hollis Road 159
Holly Mount 101
Holson, Joe 177
Home 15, 26, 28
homecoming services 72
Home Economics 102
home-made ice cream 127
homemade soups 126
home remedies 131, 132
home rule 20
Honeymooners 149
Hopkins, John M. 208, 211
Hospital for the Mentally Retarded 77
hotdogs 126
hot-water bottle 131
Hough, John 207
Howdy Doody Show 149
Howell, Robert D. 210
Hudson 159
Hudson, Henry 15
Hundreds 16, 17, 70, 179
Huntley-Brinkley Report 150
Huntley, Chet 150
Hurricane Hazel 173
hydraulic cylinder 63
Hyland Smith 116
Hymnal 71

I

Ice Cream Festivals 27, 71
ice cream freezer 127
incubators 47
Indian artifacts 33
Indian River Bay 16
Indian River Hundred 18
Indian River School District 99
Industrial Electricity 103
Industrial Park 40, 159
Industrial Park Boulevard 159
integrators 50, 89
irrigation 64

J

Jack Benny 149
James Pettyjohn's Old Field 18
Jason School 164
Jason, William C. 164
Jefferson, Myrtle 101
Jefferson, Thomas 17
Jenny 9
Jicha, Hubert F. Jr. 209
Jimmie's 4, 10, 93, 96
Jim Sabo, Esq. 181
Johnson 166
Johnson, Albert J. 208, 211
Johnson, Everett 109, 111
Johnson, Nathaniel M. 208, 211
Johnson Road 68, 69
Johnson's Society 69, 207, 213
Johnson, William M. 208
Johson, William M. 211
Joseph, Dagworthy 18
Joseph, John D. 72
Joseph, Melvin 40, 174
Joseph, Paynter (Paint) 110
Joseph's Dairy 32, 124
Joseph's milk bottle 124

K

Kaiser 159
Kawan Acres Development 100
Kee, Edwin (Ed) 7
Keeler, Mary 101
Kennedy, Robert F. 172
Kent and Sussex Fair 175
Kent County, Delaware 15
kerosene pump 108
Kersey, Lee 160
kickball 100
kickers 94
King, Gaye Pettyjohn 73, 107
King, Harold 95
Koppel, Charlie 189

L

Labor Day 43, 117
"laid away" 66
lard 55
Lawrence Welk 149
layer boxes 79
Layton, Judy 107
Layton Theater 44
"Letter" 104
Letter 104
letter sweaters 104
Lewes 15, 17, 18, 44, 99, 101, 132, 134, 179
Library Club 105

Rural Life in the 1950's and 60's

license tag 160
lima beans 95, 120, 122, 126
   bush lima beans 122
   dried lima beans 126
lime 122
Lincoln, Abraham 115
Lindsay-Hudgins, Debra 210
Lingo, Ruth 101
linseed oil 66
Little Engine That Could 188
liver 80
"London Bridge is Falling Down" 170
Lone Ranger 143
Long Neck 166
lookout towers 20
Lord Baltimore 99
Lord Calvert 16
Lord De La Warr 15
Lord's Prayer 100
Louisville Sluggers 38
Lower 3 Counties of Pennsylvannia 16
"Lower Slower Delaware." 170
Lucia, Frank 209
lunch 43, 102, 125, 166

M

Machine Shop 103
mailbox 154, 155
manure 59, 66, 122
   chicken manure 122
   stable manure 122
manure forks 59
manure spreaders 59, 66
March '62 Storm 174
March of Dimes 133
Marshall, E.H. 209
Marshall, Paige 210
Marvel Museum 7
Maryland 15, 16, 18, 19, 34, 49, 104, 148, 166, 169, 170
   Cambridge 166
   Ocean City 190
Marzoa, Ed 141
Maschauer, Dr. Carl 8
Mason, Charles 16
Mason-Dixon line 16
Masonic Lodge 100
Massey's Landing 188
McCabe, Russ 7
McClintock, W.L. 209
McCoy, Paul E. 209
McFarlane, William R. 209
McWilliams, Sam 210
Megee, Floyd 160
Megee Motors 160
Megee, Terry 160

Memorial Day 43, 117
messes 126
Methodist 19, 27, 68, 69, 73, 166, 213
Methodist Episcopal Church 19, 166, 213
Methodist Youth Fellowship 27, 73
Mid-Atlantic 15, 16
"midway" 175
Midway Theater 44
Milford 16, 31, 132, 145, 159
Milford Chronicle 145
Milford Memorial Hospital 132
military 40, 106
milk-house 85
milking stool 94
Mill and Cabinet 103
Millsboro 16, 20, 99, 100, 160, 193
Millsboro School 100
Milton 16, 20, 58, 61, 65, 99, 116, 141
mimeograph machines 103
Missipillion 17
Mississippi 169
Mom Mom Allie 70
monkey bars 100
Montgomery Wards Catalog 115
Moore Brothers 29, 46, 47, 48, 58, 185
Moore, Carlton 7, 109
Moore, Charles 73, 132
Moore, Ella M. 86
Moore, J. Everett Sr. 208
Moore, Larry W. 70, 208
Moore, Margaret 132
Moore, Merrill C. 208
Moore, Mrs. J. Everett Sr. 208
Moors 166
Morgan, L.B. 209
Morning News 83, 145, 146
Mountaire 50
mounted cornpicker 64
mousers 29
Mr. Marvel 121
Mrs. Elliott 174
Mt. Joy 109
mulch pile 122
Mumford, Alvin 107
Mumford's Sheet Metal Works 65
Murray, Aubrey 7
My Friend Flicka 149

N

Nader, Ralph 161
Nanticoke Hospital 132
Nanticoke River 16
Nanticokes 16, 166
Napan, Nuth 106
Nash-Kelvinator 159
Nassau 109

National Guard 40, 43, 174
National Honor Society 105
NBC 150, 151
neck 80
Negroes 165, 167
Newark 169
New Castle 61
New Ground District 55
Newport News, Virginia 95
New Road 28
no-eczema sunburn ointment 190
non-stick pans 125
Noon Fire Whistle 185
nor'easter 174
North Carolina 173
Norwood 166
Novocain 133

O

Oak Orchard 16, 167, 189
O'Day, Charlie 58
Odd Fellows Cemetery 61
oil 161
oilcloth apron 80
oil space heater 78, 85
Old Academy 100
Oldsmobile 159
Oliver Jones' Store 109
onion 120, 121, 122, 127
Oral Roberts "Healing Tent Crusades" 162
outside antennas 149
ox roast 179
oyster stew 127

P

Pan Spaghetti 215
party line 137
Patent Medicines 131, 133
peach basket 121
Peanut Butter Candy 216
Pennell, Pat 107
Penns 16
Pennsylvania 14, 16, 95, 166, 177, 185
Pepper, Dale 189
peppers 121
pep rallys 105
Perdue 50
Perry, Basil 57, 65, 110, 194
Perry, Betty 99
Perry, Billy 173
Perry, Bobby 99
Peru 106
   Lima 106
Peterkin's Road 159
Pettyjohn, Ralston 73

Peurifoy, Edward 209
pheasant 185
Philadelphia 19, 95, 150, 162, 188
phone booth 139
Physical Education 104
picking up sticks 56
pickled watermelon rind 95
pickups 189
Pie Road 159
Pinky Lee Show 149
Pipjenny 195
pitch and catch 37
pitcher-top hand pump 82
playground equipment 100, 117
Plays 105
plowing 30, 63, 96
Pole beans 122
polio epidemic 132
Ponshock, Stacy 7
Pontiac 159
Pony League baseball 38
pops and rollers 37
potato cakes 127
Potatoes in Bacon Water 215
potato masher 124, 127
pot luck dinners 71
poultice 131
poultry 7, 20, 47, 48, 50, 61, 62, 89, 141, 143
Poultry Auction 141, 143
Practical Nursing 103
preaching 27, 70
pregnancy 102
President Franklin Roosevelt 143
President Kennedy 102, 151, 172
Presidents Day 115
princess phone 138
printing 101
Prisoner of War camp 70
prison labor 126
Protestant 19
Providence 70, 207
PTA 102
PTO 59
Public Square 21
pull-behind combine 96
pull behind cornpicker 64
Pulleri, Dominick 128
pulpit 207
pumpkin ball 41
Purnell's Hardware 32

Q

Queen Ann style paneling 78
Quesada, Bill 182

R

rabbit hunting 42, 96
radish 122
Rafter, Di 7
rag rugs 85
raised bed garden 88
Ralph, H.M. 209
Ralph Hoebee and the Indian River Boys 142
Ralph Hoebee Show 141
Rambler 159, 160
RD 155
reading 101, 151
recess 100, 207
recycled 12, 55, 58
Redden 58
Rehoboth 17, 19, 42, 44, 47, 99, 117, 118, 128
Responsive reading 70
Return Day 179
Reverend Joe Holliday 73
Reverend John Hough 72, 213
Reverend Mulligan 107
Revolution 14, 17
Richardson, Madeline 101
Rifle Club 105
Ring Neck Pheasant 185
Rin Tin Tin 149
Road #315 28
Rocket Sled 176
Rockwell, Norman 118
rolling pin 125
Romans, M.T. 209
roosts 79
root crops 122
Root crops 121
root rakes 56
Route 155
Route 30 57, 100
Royal governor of Virginia 15
Roy Rogers Show 149
Rozelle, Jack 209
RR 155
rug beater 54
Rural Electrification Act 83
Rural Free Delivery 155, 156
Russell, Ed 47
Russell, George T. 24, 25
Rust, Harriet 211
Rust, Peter 208, 211
Rust, Raymond 106
Rust Road 159
Rust, Tommy 106
Rust, Wayne 37, 109

S

Salisbury Switch 19
Salisbury Times 145
Sandburg, Carl 188

Sandhill 207
Santa 71, 116
saplings 79, 122
sassafras pull handle 82, 83
sausage 55, 125
sawdust 59, 61, 122
Schatz, Ron 210
scoop shovels 59
scrapple 55, 125
screwdriver 103
scripture readings 70
Seaford 17, 44, 106, 132
Sears Catalog 115
secretarial 102, 103
segregation 117, 165
Selbyville 65, 99, 141
semi mounted plows 63
Senator Curt Steen 159
separate but equal 166
sermon 70, 73, 151
Service Club 105
servicemen 89
Sevin dust 122
Sharff, J. Thomas 179
Shat 194
shed style chicken house 59
sheep 93, 94, 194
sheer poles 55
shelling beans 122
S & H Green Stamp 162
S&H Green stamps 32
S&H Green Stamps 32
shillings and pence 90
shingle hatchet 58
shingle nails 58
Shockley, Marion 107
Shorthand 102
Short, Norman 189
Shultz, J. Melvin 209
Simpler Branch Road 159
Simpler, Josiah 211
Sky King 149
slab wood 81
sliced tomatoes 125, 126
slide 100
slide rules 103
slingshot 39, 40
Smith, Bob 141
Smith, Eunice 85
Smith, Harry 160
Smith, Silas 208, 211
snake 192
snapping turtle 192
Snively, Robert L. 133
softball 72, 104
soft drink 38, 110

Southern States 46, 48, 121
sow's-ear and pig tail 127
spark plugs 161
special singing 70
spelling 101
spring break 115
Springfield 10, 29, 46, 48, 68, 69, 75, 78, 92, 94, 108, 109, 111, 159, 207, 211, 213
Springfield Crossroads 68, 69, 109, 207, 213
Springfield Road 10, 29, 46, 48, 69, 78, 92, 94, 109, 111, 159
Springfield School #33 48, 69
Spry, C.W. 209
Square 24, 25
squash 122
  fried squash 126
squirrel hunt 41
squirrels 41, 85
stables 30, 76, 175
Stage Crew 105
stained glass windows 69, 73
State Fair 175
State School Board 187
Steele, Elwood (Woody) 160
Steele, Mrs. Wilmer 20
Stell Rogers' Store 109
Stewart, Lilly 77
St. Georges Bridge 170
St Georges Chapel 178
"still" 186
St. John's Quartet 73
St. John's United Methodist Church 6, 11, 57, 58, 68, 69, 70, 73, 87, 155, 160, 206, 207, 208, 209, 211
Stockley 65, 77
Stockley Center 77
St. Paul's Episcopal Church 100
strawberry 57, 120
strawberry bed 120
strawberry ticket 57
string beans 95, 122
St.Swithen's Day 194
Studebaker 65, 159, 160, 161
Student Council 105
Sturgis, William 107
Sugar corn 110
summer kitchen 81, 88
Sunday School 70, 71, 188, 208
suspension 102
Sussex Central High School 104, 132
Sussex Countian 25, 41, 145
Sussex County 11, 15, 16, 18, 20, 28, 146
Sussex Guide 145, 146
Sussex Studebaker, Co. 160
Sussex Tech 103
Sutton, J.W. 209

Svecz, Carol E. 210
Swager, Theodore 209
swamp monster 186
Swedes 15
sweep 76, 82, 83
sweet potato 116, 117, 122
swings 100
Sycamore Store 33, 58

T

tag 100
tar tape 38
tassel 110
Tastee Freeze 33, 34
Taylore, Wm.P. 209
Taylor, Harry 209
teetotallers 131
tend the chickens 60
Terramycin 48
Thailand 106
Thanksgiving 42, 111, 115, 117
The Blue Hen State 17
The Cradle of Methodism 19
The Diamond State 17
The First State 17
The Golden Herald Staff 105
The Half Moon 15
The Inlet Bridge Collapse 182
The Peach State 17
"The Pony Engine" 188
The Small Wonder 17
The Store 109
Thomas, Edwin C. 209
Thomas, George S. 209
Thompson, Chuck 150
three-bottom plow 62
three-point hitch 63
tick 192
"times" table 101
toilet 85, 208
tomato 110, 120, 121, 125, 126
Tom Best's Store 109
Townsends 50, 190
Townsend's R22 190
transistor radio 142
Trap Pond State Park 117
tricycle style front 62
Troubadour of the Eastern Shore 141
Truitt, Betty Abbott 85
Truitt, Clara 93
Truitt, F. Helen 76, 109
Truitt, Francis 48, 109
Truitt, Jimmie 7, 12, 37, 41, 58, 83, 85, 89, 92, 93, 94, 120, 123, 161, 173, 177, 189
Truitt, Jimmie Jr. 37, 41, 85, 89, 92, 93, 120, 123, 173, 177

Rural Life in the 1950's and 60's

Truitt, Jimmie Sr. 12, 42, 83, 94, 189
Truitt, Missy 85
Truitt, Noah 70, 176
Truitt, Sally 70
Truitt's Store 48, 109
trustees 126, 207, 208, 211, 213
turkey beard 116
Turnip 122
turnip greens 122
two-row corn picker 64
typewriters 102, 103
Tyson 50

U

U-boats 20
"Uncle Nat" 188
University of Delaware 169
University of Delaware Morris Library 7
Unsafe At Any Speed 161
UPS 155
"upstate" 169
U S Savings Bonds 101

V

Vanaman, Bob 107
VanBurkslow, James T. 209
vending machines 102
Vicks Vapor Rub 131
Vietnam 106, 151
Virginia 169
   Falls Church, Va 169
   Williamsburg, Va 169
Virginia Pine 82
Vocational 103
Von Goeres, Herb 107

W

WABC 142
Wade, William (Bill) 7
Walls, Eli 87, 90
Walls, Gideon 87
Wall's Homestead 4, 10, 76, 88
Walls, Ida 84
Walls, James 87
Walls, James P. 208, 211
Walls, Jimmie 181
Walls, John 211
Walls, John C. 211
Walls, Mary 86
Walls, Mr. and Mrs. Sheppard M. 77
Walls, Rosalee 7
Walls, Samuel 86, 90
Walls, Sheppard 84
Walls, Sheppard M. 72, 87
Walls, Thomas 86

Walter Cronkite 151
Warrington, Everett 58
Washington DC 150, 168
watermelon 122
   pickled watermelon 95
WBOC 7, 141, 148, 150, 151
WBOC 16 150
WBOC TV Park 148
WD45 Allis Chalmers Tractor 62
weed whip 56
Weekly Reader 101
Welding 103
well sweep 76, 83
Weslager, C.A. 166
West, Bob 73
Western Shore of Maryland 169
Westfall, Jeffrey 209
West, Harold 173
West, Jim 110
West Market Street 98, 99
West, T.A. 208
West Virginia 169
Wheaties 79, 84
whipping post 24
White, Clarke 7, 146
white oak tree 83
whole milk 125
wide-plank floors 78
Williams, Dr. William 7
Williams, W.S.H. 209
Wilmington 19, 23, 166
Wilson, Carroll 110, 116
Wilson, George A. 208
Wilson, James H. 209
Wilson, Jim 111
Wilson, Josiah S. 72
Wilson, Landis 134
Wilson, Lynette 111
Wilson, Marshall 58, 109
Wilson, Richard 110
Wilsons 50
Wilson, Sam 141
Wilson's Store 10, 11, 39, 48, 58, 69, 109, 110, 159, 184, 207
Wilson, William 207
Wilson, William (Will) 58
winding stairway 78, 86
winter break 115
Wish Books 115
WJWL 140
Woodbridge 99
wood cook stove 81
Woolworth Store 116
Workman Brothers 50
Workman's Store 109
World Book 103

World War II 20, 40, 101, 143
wreath-making 116
wrestling 104, 105
Wright, E.N. 209
Wright, Gussie 178
wringer washer 82
writing 49, 101
WSEA FM 140

Y

yard hens 93
Yearbook 105, 167
Yellow Layer Cake 216

Z

Zoar 207
Zoar Church 57, 100, 207
Zwaanendale 15

Rural Life in the 1950's and 60's